D1233651

THE
COLLECTED POEMS
OF
John Peale Bishop

JOHN PEALE BISHOP, 1942

THE
COLLECTED POEMS
OF

John Peale Bishop

EDITED WITH A PREFACE

AND A

PERSONAL MEMOIR

BY

ALLEN TATE

OCTAGON BOOKS

A DIVISION OF FARRAR, STRAUS AND GIROUX

New York　　1975

*Reprinted 1975
by special arrangement with Charles Scribner's Sons*

OCTAGON BOOKS
A DIVISION OF FARRAR, STRAUS & GIROUX, INC.
19 Union Square West
New York, N.Y. 10003

Library of Congress Cataloging in Publication Data

Bishop, John Peale, 1892-1944.
 The collected poems of John Peale Bishop.

 Reprint of the ed. published by Scribner, New York.
[PS3503.I79A17   1975]   811'.5'2   75-25779
ISBN 0-374-90644-0

COPYRIGHT NOTICES AND
ACKNOWLEDGMENTS

Acknowledgment is made to Oscar Williams for permission to use "The Submarine Bed" and "Ghouls' Wharf," copyright 1944 by Oscar Williams.

All the poems, with three exceptions, in Uncollected Early Poems 1912–17 are reprinted from *The Nassau Literary Magazine*; the exceptions are "To a Woodland Pool," "Spring Comes Down This Way Again," and "The Nassau Inn," which appeared respectively in *Harper's Weekly* (1912), *The Nassau Herald* (1917), and the *Princeton Alumni Weekly* (1917).

The poems in Uncollected Early Poems 1917–1923 were first printed in *Vanity Fair*, with these exceptions: "Two Esquimaux Love Songs," "A Small Oration to the Sun," and "Always from My First Boyhood," in *Playboy* (1923); "To Helen" and "Epithalamium," in *S4N*.

The poems included in Uncollected Later Poems 1937–1945, first appeared in the following magazines and books:

"Resurrection" in *Furioso* (Summer, 1941); "The Hours" in *The Nation* (March 3, 1941); "The Parallel" and "The Spare Quilt" in *Poetry: A Magazine of Verse* (April, 1944); "The Dream" in *The Sewanee Review* (Winter, 1945); "A Subject of Sea Change" in *The American Scholar* (April, 1943); "Occupation of a City" in *Decision* (March, 1941); "A Charm" in *Fantasy* (No. 4, 1937). Also in Section IV are "Ghouls' Wharf" and "The Submarine Bed," which were first printed in the anthology *New Poems 1944*, edited by Oscar Williams (Howell, Soskin, 1944).

Bishop's translations, reprinted here as a separate section, were first published as follows: "Then Twist the Neck of This Delusive Swan" and "The Peasant Declares His Love" in *Anthology of Contemporary Latin American Poetry*, edited by Dudley Fitts (New Directions, 1942); all translations except those just named were included in *Now With His Love* or *Selected Poems*.

"John Peale Bishop: A Personal Memoir" appeared in *The Western Review*, Winter 1948.

A. T.

✒§ PREFACE §✑

CRITICAL EDITION OF THE POEMS OF A MAN SO RECENTLY dead as John Peale Bishop is not possible at the present time; nor would it, I think, be desirable. The aim of this collection is to bring to a larger public a more complete view of his poetry than any of his books reached in his lifetime. But the reader will observe that the title of the present volume is the *Collected* (not the Complete) *Poems* of John Peale Bishop. Had an even more thorough search been made than I had time or talent to make, completeness would have been impossible, even a delusion, against which literary history affords many warnings. And it seemed to me improper to include more than a representative selection from the *juvenilia*. At a later time, perhaps, some other editor, possessing the gift and patience of scholarship and, one hopes, the critical gift also, will give us the critical edition that every poet with any claim to the interest of posterity is entitled to have.

The sources of this volume are chiefly the published books, the files of magazines, and the posthumous papers of the poet. (I am grateful to Mrs. Margaret Hutchins Bishop, the poet's widow, for the promptness with which she delivered the papers into my hands.) The manuscripts were much more numerous than I had any reason to expect. There were hundreds of sheets covered with notes for poems, with lines, phrases, unfinished stanzas, with endless different versions of these, some with so many interlineations and variant readings that reconstruction in all but a few instances was impossible. The difficulty was increased by the

vii

all but illegible hand of the poet. I think it is safe to say that, in spite of the difficulties, I have not missed a completed poem; or perhaps I had better say I have not omitted a single unpublished poem that existed in a version which critical propriety, rather than the vanity of editorial ingenuity, could pronounce tolerably finished. I had to take the responsibility of choosing one among several readings of a line or a stanza; but since this is not a critical edition, it would not be appropriate to set down here the defense of my choices The manuscripts will be preserved, and my faulty judgment can be corrected in due time. Lest I appear to exaggerate this matter, I should point out that the problem of choice arose in not more than a dozen lines, in about eight poems; these, I need scarcely say, are all to be found in the two sections of "Unpublished Poems."

Besides the main sources there were two others: Mr. Edmund Wilson's papers, which he very kindly searched, and my own. Mr. Wilson gave me several unpublished poems that I had not seen, and I found two others in the large collection of letters that Bishop had written to me between 1928 and his death in 1944. It is possible that both Mr. Wilson and I will find other poems later on. Mr. Archibald MacLeish was not sure that his correspondence with Bishop had been preserved; at any rate it was not accessible. (Mr. Wilson, Mr. MacLeish, and I seem to have been his principal literary correspondents after 1925.) It was his custom to send me his poems, as it was my custom to send him mine, in manuscript, for critical comment.

A word about the plan of this book may be useful to the reader. It is in two large divisions, "Later Poems" and "Early Poems." The former comprises six sections, including his two most important books, *Now With His Love* (1933) and *Minute Particulars* (1935), exactly as he arranged them; these are the two first sections. The third contains only those poems appearing in *Selected Poems* (1941) which had not appeared in the two preceding volumes. In making up the *Selected Poems*, Bishop revised certain poems from the volumes of 1933 and 1935; I have used the revised versions * but kept them in the places where the earlier versions appeared in the earlier books. *Now With His Love* contained a separate section of translations; these I have put with his other translations, published elsewhere, in a separate section of this volume, so that his skill as a translator may be more conspicuous. The second division of the book contains two sections of "Uncollected Early Poems"; this arrangement seemed desirable as a way of isolating those poems which are clearly *juvenilia* (1912–1917) from the poems of early maturity. In this second part also appears Bishop's first book entire, *Green Fruit* (1917). There was an interval of sixteen years before he published another.

Each division of the book is in chronological order. "Later Poems" begins with the first collection of his maturity, *Now With His Love*, and ends with the group of "Translations," which were done in the last twenty years. "Early Poems" begins with selections from the uncollected *juvenilia* (1912–1917); these are followed by the volume *Green Fruit*, which brings the first period to a close. Every poem has been assigned a date. The dates of the uncollected poems are those of first magazine publication. The dating of the unpublished poems is highly conjectural in all but a few cases: here Mr. Wilson was very helpful; but on the whole I had to rely upon memory, "internal evidence," or mention of the poems in Bishop's letters to me. The dating of the poems from the books or from magazines was easier: this information is in the excellent bibliography by Mr. J. Max Patrick and Mr. Robert Stallman, published just in time for my use, in the *Princeton University Library Chronicle* (February, 1946).

Altogether John Peale Bishop published four volumes of poetry over a period of twenty-four years. He collaborated with

---

* In many poems in *Now With His Love* the lines do not begin with capital letters. In three poems—"Speaking of Poetry," "In the Dordogne," and "And When the Net Was Unwound Venus Was Found Ravelled With Mars"— I have retained this feature, though Bishop used initial capitals when he reprinted the poems in *Selected Poems*. To my eye, in these three poems, the initial capitals break the rhythms and slow down the movement of the verse. Otherwise the texts follow the versions in *Selected Poems*.

Mr. Wilson in a book of verse and prose fiction, *The Undertaker's Garland* (1922), but none of Bishop's work in this book can be called mature; it has only a "period" interest, though there are passages of great promise. He published two books of prose fiction: *Many Thousands Gone* (1931) and *Act of Darkness* (1935). As an editor he collaborated with me in collecting the anthology *American Harvest: Twenty Years of Creative Writing in the United States* (1942).

Without the help of Mr. Wilson, who knows Bishop's early work better than anybody else, and the help of Mr. Patrick and Mr. Stallman, who sent me copies of poems from obscure magazines, the editing of this book would have been not only more difficult but long delayed. I owe thanks to Mr. Willard Thorp of Princeton University; Mr. Thorp supervised the copying out of poems from *The Nassau Literary Magazine,* and so saved me much time. I am grateful to Mr. Brinley Rhys, editorial assistant of *The Sewanee Review,* for making a fair copy of most of the manuscript. I have already referred to Mrs. Bishop's kindness; I am grateful to her for letting me edit the poetry of her husband, who was my great friend. Mrs. Bishop felt none of the hesitation, nor desire for delay, with which the families of men of letters frequently obstruct the collection of their works. The late Maxwell Perkins and Mr. John Hall Wheelock, of Charles Scribner's Sons, agreed without question, a few days after Bishop's death, to publish this book. With the publication of the uncollected miscellaneous prose, edited by Mr. Wilson, the principal works of John Peale Bishop will have been made available in their entirety

A. T.

JOHN PEALE BISHOP

A PERSONAL MEMOIR

BY

ALLEN TATE

ON THE EVENING OF SEPTEMBER 23, 1925, I WAS DINING WITH Hart Crane in a speakeasy on Washington Place in New York. Towards the end of dinner I saw Kenneth Burke and another man at the far end of the restaurant; and when Crane left for another engagement I went over to speak to Burke. He introduced me to John Peale Bishop. I remember the time and circumstances because Burke made a joke about my having become a father on that day. I was a little excited and concerned with myself; I remember very little of Bishop from the hour I sat at their table. I could not suspect then that that meeting was the beginning of a long and affectionate friendship. We did not meet again until 1928, in Paris.

John Peale Bishop was born in Charles Town, West Virginia, in the Shenandoah Valley, on May 21, 1892, the son of Jonathan Peale Bishop * and Margaret Miller Cochran. On his mother's side he came of stock that had settled in Virginia in the late seventeenth and early eighteenth centuries. This Tidewater ancestry, moving westward at about the close of the French and Indian War to what was then the frontier in the Valley of Vir-

---

* The editors of *The Princeton University Library Chronicle*, in the biographical sketch accompanying the bibliography by Mr. Stallman and Mr. Patrick, have the name wrong: *John* for *Jonathan* (*The Princeton University Library Chronicle*, Vol. VII, No. 2, p. 55).

ginia, mingled with the new German and Scotch-Irish strains that had begun to pour into the Valley from Pennsylvania and the Carolinas just before the Revolution. His mother carried with her two centuries of the history of Virginia. At fourteen John copied from Waddell's *Annals of Augusta County* the names of his family connections that had fought in the Indian wars and the Revolution: Moffett, Warwick, Breckinridge, McDowell, Mc-Clanahan. With these Scotch and English families the Germans were mingled; the Millers, or Müllers, had founded in the late 1750's the town of Müllerstadt, later Woodstock, in Shenandoah County, in the lower, northern end of the Valley. But Bishop's father was of Connecticut descent, and had been brought as a child to Charles Town, where, I suppose, he always remained an outsider, being a Yankee. Bishop's beautiful poem "Beyond Connecticut, Beyond the Sea" recovers an ancestral past from which his Southern upbringing had cut him off. Years ago he told me that when a boy his father had been "stoned in the streets." The phrase appears in this poem. In Bishop there was a deep conflict of loyalties felt by many people in the border South from 1865 to 1914, and I think it is one key to the understanding of his work.

He was nine when his father died, and his mother soon remarried. In his last ten years it seemed to me, when we talked about such matters, as we more and more did, that he more and more took imaginatively the part of his father, of the outsider, of the *déraciné*. It was a rôle that merged very early in his life with that of the modern romantic poet. That he was fully conscious of the historical beginnings of this split in loyalty (it became later the condition of his special sensibility, liberating his powers of observation) is quite plain in the fine story "Many Thousands Gone," in which the Yankee officer occupying the Virginia town of Mordington (Charles Town) is himself a native of Mordington who has taken the side of the "enemy." He is described as having sandy hair, a small moustache, and a foxlike face. I have always seen in this portrait a caricature of Bishop himself.

His boyhood seems to have been that of most boys in a small Southern town. At an early age he became interested in birds and before he was ten he had written a birdbook, the manuscript of which his sister has preserved. It became a lifelong interest. In his last years he always took his field glasses when he went walking, and the sea birds of Cape Cod were a constant delight to him. He discovered an aquatic bird long supposed by ornithologists to be extinct. His sister, Mrs. Allen Myers, tells me that John, when he was a schoolboy, "declaimed poetry at all hours" and knew hundreds of lines; in high school he won an oratorical contest. I can see in this the origin of his pleasure in speaking well, and in the interminable, "elevated" talk of the Southern family at the turn of the century perhaps the origin of the noble diction of his verse: like the other Southern poets of his generation he was something of a rhetorician who never felt the influences here or abroad which later made possible the more colloquial language of the British poets Auden and MacNeice. His sister recalls the good times he had when he was young—the round of parties and dances in Charles Town and the towns nearby: in later years he told her that he didn't know whether all the girls he knew in his boyhood were pretty, but he thought they were.

His education after the elementary stage was all in the North. He attended the Mercersburg Academy in Pennsylvania, and was graduated from Princeton in 1917 when he was twenty-five. He was thus older than his friends Wilson and Fitzgerald, and his undergraduate writings, though derivative, have a precision and finish that undergraduates seldom achieve. In the First World War he was a First Lieutenant of Infantry, in the 84th Division, and remained in Europe until 1919 in command of a detachment guarding German prisoners. When he came back he went on *Vanity Fair*, later succeeding Edmund Wilson as managing editor. Between 1919 and 1922 he wrote the verse and prose pieces which became his part in *The Undertaker's Garland* (1922). On June 17, 1922, he was married to Margaret Grosvenor Hutchins, of a Columbus, Ohio, family, and went to live abroad, in Paris and Sorrento: in this period he first knew Ezra Pound, E. E. Cummings, and Archibald MacLeish. It was his first residence abroad, and more than his earlier war experience it sharpened his sense of the relation of America to Europe, and even of the relation of the South to the North. Here began the consciousness of the past in the present out of which grew his most important work. From 1924 to 1925 he was again in New York, on the staff of Paramount Pictures. In 1926 he returned to France, settling in an old house about twenty kilometers to the northeast of Paris—the Château du Petit Tressancourt in the village of Orgèval. There the Bishops lived some seven years, and my own frequent visits to Tressancourt between 1928 and 1930, and again in 1932, made it obvious to me that he had not been happy in that charming isolation. More dependent upon a sympathetic literary society than most writers, he seemed in that period remote and without concentration, except at intervals when he produced, in a burst of energy, a group of poems or an occasional story. It was my impression that he felt he ought to produce a popular work: I think he worked for a while at a musical comedy. A wit of the Bishops' circle said to me one day that "John is like a man lying in a warm bath who faintly hears the telephone ringing downstairs."

This was his condition when I arrived in Paris in 1928. On a December evening of that year he read to Robert Penn Warren and me a story, the first draft of "Many Thousands Gone," and I asked him: "Has anybody seen it?" "No," he said. I knew that his friends were constantly bringing him their work, but apparently nobody read his. He had a special modesty and detachment and a generosity which people took for granted in that time of highly developed literary "personalities" and competitive literary careers. In the twenties, in Paris and New York, few people read anything, even the books which presumably had made the reputations of the writers most talked about. I am not the right person to go into this mystery of literary fashion; yet I ought to say that John Bishop was distinctly not the fashion. He had little gift for

dramatizing himself as a literary personality, and I always sus-
pected that his dandyism, a sort of social mask behind which he
concealed himself, was his way of withdrawing from the literary
scene, perhaps an expression of contempt for the literary *arriviste*.
(This mask, of course, had its own defects; I think it limited his
range as a writer.) His closest friends at that time, Hemingway,
Fitzgerald, and MacLeish, were distinctly not *arrivistes*. Yet I felt
that nobody in Paris quite took him seriously as a writer. The
writings of all these men, and of others, including myself, would
have been the poorer without his disinterested advice: he had a
quick, intuitive sense of the problems involved in his friends'
work.

In 1933 the Bishops returned to America to live, first in New
Orleans for a year, then in Connecticut; and in 1938 they built a
house at South Chatham, Massachusetts, on Cape Cod, where
they lived until John's death in 1944. Here he lived again in the
isolation that he had known at Orgèval. Between 1936, when
Minute Particulars appeared, and 1940, when Scott Fitzgerald
died, he produced very little poetry, yet he wrote in those years
some of his best critical essays, "The Discipline of Poetry," "The
Sorrows of Thomas Wolfe," and "Poetry and Painting." The
death of Fitzgerald was the occasion of the elegy "The Hours"
and indirectly of numerous short poems which are among his best,
as well as the fine long poem "A Subject of Sea Change." Early
in 1941 he came to New York as Publications Director of the
Office of the Coordinator of Inter-American Affairs, where he
planned and put through some of the best South American an-
thologies; here he invited me to collaborate with him in a United
States anthology to be translated into Spanish for the South
American republics; and I saw him constantly. He seemed in the
year and a half he thus spent in New York to regain something of
his old enthusiasm for literature (I had felt a withdrawal in the
two or three years before 1941), but his health was not good and
the high blood pressure that he had had for many years was get-
ting worse. He went back to South Chatham in June, 1942.

In the next year and a half I did not see him, being in the South; but when I saw him again, in November, 1943, he had aged greatly. It is not too much to say that the war hastened his death. Not being a man of action, he had few of the public outlets which some of his old friends seized to get themselves through the inner crisis which the war created in us all. But this is not the place to go into this matter and I leave it to other commentators. In October, 1943, I had suggested to Archie MacLeish, who was then Librarian of Congress, that John would be the right man to fill the new post of Resident Fellow in Comparative Literature in the Library; and MacLeish acted at once. But when John arrived in Washington early in November he was obviously ill. At the end of two weeks he had a heart attack and had to go home. I put him on the train, and had I known how ill he was I should have gone with him. After a few weeks he seemed to get better, and late that winter was able to walk a little; but in March he grew weaker and by the middle of March his wife knew that the end was not far away. A few days before he died Margaret telephoned me and I asked her whether it might please John to have me sit with him: she told me that he could no longer recognize me or anybody else. On April 4, 1944, he died.

About a week before his death, becoming conscious for a while, he told Margaret that he had been blessed with "wonderful friends" and that his life had not been wasted. We who survive him into a world that he could not have liked are, I think, even better judges of that than he. The names of the friends he mentioned in the last conscious hour it pleases me to set down as he spoke them to his wife: "Bunny, Allen, and Archie." Not least among John's gifts was the gift of distinguished friendship. In that same talk he dictated to Margaret his epitaph:

> Long did I live
> Consistent, lonely, proud.
> Not death, but fear of death,
> Restores us to the crowd.

✑ CONTENTS ॐ

THE
COLLECTED POEMS
OF
John Peale Bishop

LATER POEMS

NOW WITH HIS LOVE
1933

NOW WITH HIS LOVE

SPEAKING OF POETRY

The ceremony must be found
that will wed Desdemona to the huge Moor.

It is not enough—
to win the approval of the Senator
or to outwit his disapproval; honest Iago
can manage that: it is not enough. For then,
though she may pant again in his black arms
(his weight resilient as a Barbary stallion's)
she will be found
when the ambassadors of the Venetian state arrive
again smothered. These things have not been changed,
not in three hundred years.

(Tupping is still tupping
though that particular word is obsolete.
Naturally, the ritual would not be in Latin.)

For though Othello had his blood from kings
his ancestry was barbarous, his ways African,
his speech uncouth. It must be remembered
that though he valued an embroidery—
three mulberries proper on a silk like silver—
it was not for the subtlety of the stitches,
but for the magic in it. Whereas, Desdemona

5

once contrived to imitate in needlework
her father's shield, and plucked it out
three times, to begin again, each time
with diminished colors. This is a small point
but indicative.

        Desdemona was small and fair,
delicate as a grasshopper
at the tag-end of summer: a Venetian
to her noble finger tips.

        O, it is not enough
that they should meet, naked, at dead of night
in a small inn on a dark canal. Procurers
less expert than Iago can arrange as much.

The ceremony must be found

Traditional, with all its symbols
ancient as the metaphors in dreams;
strange, with never before heard music; continuous
until the torches deaden at the bedroom door.

1925

THE TRUTH ABOUT THE DEW

Maybe she dreamed the colonnade:
    But surely, surely, she has seen
Magnolias drenched in moonlit shade.
    Maria sees the dew as green.

Burdened Calinda totes the sun
    Bundle-headed to her shack;
Her arms are black in unison,
    Her shoulders bare. Here dew is black.

6

But Abner hoeing hillside corn
  Swipes his wet hair to clear his sight.
The sun is hilled. He could have sworn
  Dew on the long corn leaves was white.

This morning, however, a small
  Lascivious rabbit, looking through
A cobweb, shivered and let fall
  Myriads of rainbows from the dew.

1932

PORTRAIT OF MRS. C

Aetatis suae 75

                    Where I was born
The gardens were all terraces and the grapevines
Ran everywhere; that shrivelled and turned brown
At the first frost, were raked
And burned in piles: the dead leaves.
The river bottoms drifted like smoke
And the woods, the woods, were yellow as bonfires
In the fall—in the hunting season
When even the slaves fed upon partridge.
The mornings were cold. I used to run
Down to the nearest cabin and climb into bed
With my nigger mammy. It was warm there.
But this place falls to rack and ruin;
What can I do with these rapscallion blacks
That want three dollars just to clean the yard.
I am alone. No one. Not even a negro girl
To bring the wood in and to fix the fires.

Margaret is dead, my Margaret. . . . And Margaret's Margaret
Married, has a house at Rye,

7

Travels with a maid, goes abroad each year,
To a Mr. Mouskowitz.
I think he must be a Pole.

That would be nothing to you. But I am old,
An old woman. Sometimes I wonder, what if I fall?
In fear and trembling, fall on the staircase?
I climb at night to an empty room. I stop
On the stairs. I cannot breathe. I hear—
And my heart beats so.

                    Once I fell
Here on the hearthstone, leaning
To lay the fires, fell with the firewood
Still in my arms; fell and could not call;
Only thought:
Who is it will find me after days and days
My head against the grate and the ashes in my hair?

You must not think me shiftless. I know this room . . .
Haircloth was once elegant. The rest is gone,
The portraits and the consoles: Lettice Buckworth
Whom we thought a Lely; Banister Owen
In the buff-satin waistcoat, three buttons undone
And the brownish sheep in the background; all but one
My great-aunt in the oval over your head,
Maria Boys, who took to her bed still young,
Who had her slaves brought to her side there
And whipped until they bled.

                    Her cupboard stood
Chock-full of candied fruit, shoes she had never worn.
Those were her eyes the Negroes dreaded,
Coming to her from the sun. . . . She died—
I've heard—still beautiful, tossing her tester bed,
From surfeit of peaches on a winter night.

8

When did you last see Margaret? Not my Margaret—
You knew that she was dead—but Margaret's Margaret?
She came in a great hurry, came
To borrow my wedding veil, the low-heeled
Yellow shoes I'd worn. I thought it strange.

—Who is this man? What is his name?

They'd met, it seems,
At a banquet, a fashionable affair, and all the men
Applauded when she sang—some witty trifle,
A little mischievous.

                    —And the following day
He followed you to the seashore?
                           I was confused.

—O Grandmother! Don't act like you were cracked.
He's money enough. There was plenty of champagne.
You can't get men sitting with folded hands
And never crossing your knees. The sixties went out
When the seventies came in.

                         I looked at her
Severely. Then I said: O, it's nothing to me
That you are beautiful, nothing
That you are young! We too
Could take the young men by the ears! We
Could sit still and put on quiet airs, could
Drop our hands and smooth out folds and yet
Lose nothing.

           She only stared
Upon the keyboard. She only said:
I think I'll take the wedding veil.

—We did not do such things when I was young!

I saw her stare
As though she would have played a tune
Touching her fingers to the yellow keys
But was afraid of dust. And dust—
Not music—was the sound she made.

Today I received a little dun:
Some little purchases from a Mr. Baum.
And the boy came to the front door, stood there,
One foot in my hallway, would not leave.
What could I say to such effrontery?
I shoved the door. We never talked of money—
Not when I was young!

                    For God in Heaven!
What is there to this life unless we can
Endow it with some rarity beyond
The common run? And we who in Green Spring
Had little—were left and lost at last
With little but our names—at least could show
Some elegance of hand, of foot, of voice,
Some sense, when the times hit, of what we were,
Some stubbornness that held
Against the worst vicissitudes of pride.

The land where I was born is in Albemarle.
                    And I have seen the soldiers there
And the ladies took their wedding gowns
And tore them into shreds. Stood in the streets
And knelt upon the kerbs, to bind their wounds
And bind their poor blood-matted heads. But you
Have been a soldier and you know
How some of them were young!
                    And then

My brothers went to Norfolk, played the races,
Made a living for the livery stables, bet
Their bottom dollar, lost, came home, laughed
And swore they still had something left to lose
And showed their empty pockets.

                             We were lost
Without the land, tatterdemalion, proud;
Absurd, no doubt, in our futility
And fine, I do not doubt, too fine,
In the discrimination of despair.

After the war, my grandfather used to go
Down past the stables and in the carriage shed
Mount to his father's father's coach and in the dark
For hours sit motionless; old,
Behind small windows of square glass; and while his fingers
Strayed to more exhausted fringes
The yellow silk, he'd bow to crowds
Of people who, I think, were dead.

A green glass coach shaped like a fairy tale.
She took the veil, the slippers were too small.

It does not matter that she thinks me
A foolish old woman, half-daft, fit only
For a modest funeral. I do not care.
I said I do not care. And yet, at times,
She fills me with more cold
Than all the creaking of this lonely house.

Margaret's Margaret!

                    I have not forgotten
How she sat—and she was old:

Mrs. Wyvern
Upright by the firescreen, stiff with vehemence,
And wielding her turkey-feather fan, talked
As though she would have talked down night and death
With good sound common sense. You see!—and her fan—
My life has not been uneventful! And when
Her brother stirred the coals, I hope
There's nothing common about us!
They did the cooking between them, while he
Pasted his coat-of-arms in his hatcrown.

Ah, no! There's something I have no more lost
Than I have lost (although I've given my pew up)
Faith in God! But when I die, she'll say,
It is too far to come. She took
The veil. The slippers were too small.

Nebuchadnezzar the King of the Jews
Went to Heaven in his old gumshoes

I've heard the niggers singing in the time
Of cornshucking when they'd made a blaze
Of cornstalks. And Many thousands gone.

From his name I think he must be a Pole.

1933

IN THE DORDOGNE

We stood up before day
and shaved by metal mirrors
in the faint flame of a faulty candle.

And we hurried down the wide stone stairs
with a clirr of spur chains

12

on stone. And we thought
when the cocks crew
that the ghosts of a dead dawn
would rise and be off. But they stayed
under the window, crouched on the staircase,
the window now the color of morning.

The colonel slept in the bed of Sully
slept on: but we descended
and saw in a niche in the white wall
a Virgin and child, serene
who were stone: we saw sycamores:
three aged mages
scattering gifts of gold.
But when the wind blew, there were autumn odors
and the shadowed trees
had the dapplings of young fawns.

And each day one died or another
died: each week we sent out thousands
that returned by hundreds
wounded or gassed. And those that died
We buried close to the old wall
within a stone's throw of Perigord
under the tower of the troubadours.

And because we had courage;
because there was courage and youth
ready to be wasted; because we endured
and were prepared for all endurance;
we thought something must come of it:
that the Virgin would raise her child and smile;
the trees gather up their gold and go;
that courage would avail something
and something we had never lost

be regained through wastage, by dying,
by burying the others under the English tower.

The colonel slept on in the bed of Sully
under the ravelling curtains: the leaves fell
and were blown away: the young men rotted
under the shadow of the tower
in a land of small clear silent streams
where the coming on of evening is
the letting down of blue and azure veils
over the clear and silent streams
delicately bordered by poplars.

1933

AND WHEN THE NET WAS UNWOUND VENUS WAS FOUND RAVELLED WITH MARS

Out of the dark came fat eyes
and shuffling along the corridor
what darkness let become a face: when lifted
bristled like a boar's and bit
with one tooth on the lower lip. I spoke
and could not hear my words. She heard
and turned upon the banister.

In black silk her bosom seemed
taking flight for heaven in heaviest breath
upon the stairs, her strange feet
made no sound upon the stairs. I heard—
to tell the truth it was my heart I heard
climbing that made that sound.

She stopped us with a sound of keys
who might have climbed forever.

She stooped then with a noise of keys
to rattle upon a door that opened
upon the bed together.

There were trees
that leaned upon the window frame. We stood
in dusk of adulterous crimson and her stare.

Over the bed in dusty crimson hung
a sprig of blessed wood, deceased in green
and dead upon the walls. I heard her smile:
I saw those feet that padded on the floor-tiles
still without sound. We were not the first—
Ah, not the first, Madam! to bed
Between those sheets . . . I think I must have paid
with something like despair. I said,
In truth, that toothed fang
Could gnaw a thread like time's. But she was gone.

And after a long touch of arms
I plead, *Do you like love?* She answered *Love?*
I kept my thought all thinking on one point
that burned upon my thighs, until it seemed
the very center whence they wheel, all fiery
and all turning stars. We stopped them on a kiss.

I was the first to nakedness. Suddenly she
left her dress and her feet were on the floor.
It seemed her body had been burned
by blue Italian ponds
and moving kept such equipoise as though
she had learned of old bronze
bright breast and the thigh like a boy's.

What did we then?
What did we then in that young season?

Wordless throats, maddened mouths, crying skins?
I only know what then she did to me.

I only know that all was done
with perfect lust, that died and came again,
Proserpine that came again
with spring, after winter, came with white
and yellow flowers to scatter Aetna
with white and yellow flowers and at last
brought sleep.

      We had not known
the afternoon was going, when waking
evening was green and the mirror held the sky.
Laughing we waked
in arms, we lay
the time it takes to make a star.

This was in the time of the long war
when the old deliberated and always rose
to the same decision: More of the young
must die.

      Of them I remember and their nights
her warmth as of a million suns.

1933

YOUNG MEN DEAD

Bernard Peyton is dead
It is thirteen years:
Son of a decayed house
He might have made his roof
Less contumelious
Had there been time enough
Before they buried his bed;

Now it is thirteen years
At seventeen years old.
And Mooch of the bull-red
Hair who had so many dears
Enjoyed to the core
And Newlin who hadn't one
To answer his shy desire
Are blanketed in the mould
Dead in the long war.
And I who have most reason
Remember them only when the sun
Is at his dullest season.

1933

COLLOQUY IN A GARDEN

"Is it a door you want?"
                                    "A corridor
That opens upward like a grave."
"Why have you never asked for this before?"
"O, but I have!"

"Why do you groping go with blinded eyes
Halting where earth's a hollow sound?"
"I have long known the way to paradise
Was underground."

1932

STILL LIFE: CARROTS

Tritons
Just rising from the uneven wave, until
Their seaweed hair had twice appeared, balancing
Above the wave, who stood, might have displayed
Thoughts such as these:

                              Rude seagods who smiled
Being young and sunned at times
Among the rocks—rough crags prodigious thrust
Into the intensest blue that trembles
Upward from the warm Aegean.

1933

ODE

Why will they never sleep
Those great women who sit
Peering at me with parrot eyes?
They sit with grave knees; they keep
Perpetual stare; and their hands move
As though hands could be aware—
Forward and back, to begin again—
As though on tumultous shuttles of wind they wove
Shrouds out of air.

The three are sisters. There is one
Who sits divine in weeping stone
On a small chair of skeleton
And is most inescapable.
I have walked through many mirrors
But always accompanied.
I have been as many men, as many ghosts,
As there are days. The boy was seen
Always at rainfall, mistily, not lost.
I have tried changing shapes
But always, alone, I have heard
Her shadow coming nearer, and known
The awful grasp of striding hands
Goddess! upon
The screaming metamorphosis.

One has a face burned hard
As the red Cretan clay,
Who wears a white torso scarred
With figures like a calendar.
She sits among broken shafts
Of stone; she is and still will be
Who feeds on cities, gods and men
Weapons of bronze and curious ornaments
Reckoning the evens as the odds.
Her least movement recalls the sea.

The last has idiot teeth
And a brow not made
For any thoughts, but suffering.
Tired, she repeats
In idiot singing
A song shaped like a ring:
"Now is now and never Then
Dead Virgins will bear no men
And now that we speak of love, of love,
The woman's beneath
That's burdened with love
And the man's above
While the thing is done and done.
One is one and Three is three
Children may come from a spark in the sun
But One is one and never Three
And never a Virgin shall bear a Son
While the shadow lasts of the gray ashtree!"

Phantasmal marbles!
There was One who might have saved
Me from the grave dissolute stones
And parrot eyes. But He is dead,
Christ is dead. And in a grave

Dark as a sightless skull He lies
And of His bones are charnels made.

1932

METAMORPHOSES OF M

I

I have seen your feet gilded by morning
Naked under your long gown. I have seen them
Keep such state upon the unswept floor
I could have sworn Venetian artisans
Had all night been awake, painting in gold,
To set your beauty on appropriate heels.
What wonder then that I insist on gilt
As covering for your feet, which might inlay
(If there were still such metamorphoses)
The morning and form a constellation
To take all eyes from Venus, though she stood
As from antiquity in naked light
Till then unvying queen.

II

Your beauty is not used. Though you have lain
A thousand nights upon my bed, you rise
Always so splendidly renewed that I have thought,
Seeing the sweet continence of your breast,
Mole-spotted, your small waist, and long slim thigh,
That even the unicorn that savage beast
If he should startle on you fresh from light
Would be so marvelled by virginity
That he would come, trotting and mild,
To lay his head upon your fragrant lap
And be surprised.

1933

TWELFTH NIGHT

All night I thought on those wise men who took
A midnight leave of towers and came peering
Pyramidally down to the dark guards
And stared apart, each with a mad, hid look
Twitching his mummied beard
                                while the night swords
Conferred and chains fell and the unwieldy bar
Slid and swung back
                        then wandered out to name
The living demon of an unnamed star.

All night I followed them and came at last
On a low hutch propped in an alleyway
And stretched aside
                        while one by one they passed
Those stilted mages mitred in stiff blue
Under the sagging beams and through the stalls.

Following, through stench and misty fug I saw
And nothing were clearer in the scrupulous day
The rigid drooping of their ancient palls
Burnish with light, where on a toss of straw
Swaddled in rags, to their abashment, lay
Not the pedantic god whose name they knew
But a small child petulant with cries.
With courtesies unperturbed and slow
They laid their gifts down, unburnt scents and gold:
But gray evasions shamed their skeptic eyes
And the starved hands were suddenly boned with cold
As plucking their gorgeous skirts they shook to go.

1923

21

EASTER MORNING

But when he had spoken out, then I could go.
When was truth heard alone?
Even the sons of gods speaking say false.
I saw him where he stood
And when we went both had our lines of spears.

But stand apart and do not stay. Listen
But do not stay: for then, alone,
Washing the hands, letting the red blood
Flow in water, then and then only,
You may startle to hear
The unjust dark tremble into words.

The slave was standing by the closet
Door. I was alone.
This just man never heard the truth.
Truth is a sepulchre, dust is not justice,
Nor will the metaphysical toil of spiders
Conserve the shroud that hides decaying bones.
This we know in our retirement.
We must consent to let the crowd with hot
Clamor and clapping of heaved hands take choice
Of christs, thieves, blasphemers. I was not asked
To choose. Caesar shall have no riot.

Procula is distraught, cannot sleep
Or rather sleeps to shriek in dreams.
Tonight, I too turned in my rest
And roused to stare upon an arm.
It was but the deceiving cock I heard
Crowing for dawn. It was still dark.
Only on the East, I through the window saw
The deepening of the extreme blue

That brightens stars before they fade.
Today begins another Jewish week.

1933

AUTHORITY

No soul endures, Aquinas says,
Without experience of delight:
So those deprived of the Sun's rays
Seek comfort in erotic night.

1933

EPITHALAMIUM

When first my beloved came to my bed
It was as though the midnight had seen pass
Morning on the march or that great bird of the
Dayspring, newly mewed, plumed in loud brass.

My breath abandoned me and my breath failed
And silence came all sighing to my mouth.
My knees went down before her naked feet.
Love was the cry recovered me from death.

1923

WISH IN THE DAYTIME

I have so dark a need to be alone
That I would walk naked into a wood
Darker than day with tall trees, the sun
There a light once dreamt of but unknown;
And there strip burdensome flesh from the bone
And drop myself down, a sentient skeleton,

That would not hear the heart's beat, nor the blood,
But would lie still, still, in a brown shroud
Of dead leaves the rain had left, of clotted mould
Of mushrooms and colder earth, until the old
Nodding of night to day had three times bowed
In silence over the shrill trouble of men;
And then rise up and put on flesh again.

1933

FIAMETTA

Fiametta walks under the quincebuds
    In a gown the color of flowers;
Her small breasts shine through the silken stuff
    Like raindrops after showers.
The green hem of her dress is silk, but duller
Than her eyes' green color.

Her shadow restores the grass's green—
    Where the sun had gilded it;
The air has given her copper hair
    The sanguine that was requisite.
Whatever her flaws, my lady
Has no fault in her young body.

She leans with her long slender arms
    To pull down morning upon her—
Fragrance of quince, white light and falling cloud.
    The day shall have lacked due honor
Until I shall have rightly praised
Her standing thus with slight arms upraised.

1923

DOWN!

I have plucked a bough from della Vigna's thorn
And the leaves are eaten away.
The stock groans, streaming my hand with blood.
Must I delay
Till the black lean bitches come loping out of the wood
Foaming with sanguine, crashing the branches of blackthorn?

Rather stay here where bodily delight
And the body's pain
Are endlessly removed! There are narrower circles and more
Profound torments. But here the lonely escape disdain.
I have looked on that man's body who bore
On my beloved and to her delight.
1923

THIS IS THE MAN

This is the man who bore his shoulders hunched
  And arched his backbone like an angry cat;
    He also wore, derisively, a hat
A low black Jewish hat, battered and punched
Out of all argument, with his ears conched
    Beneath it, small and strangely disparate;
      His lips skimmed back upon a smile that spat
Between his toothpick and a tooth. He scrunched

Along the pathway toward us and without
    Lifting his feet went past us with the smile
      Still pinned there by the toothpick and
Just at that moment turned. Semitic snout
    Returned and upturned eyes came back, and while
      I stared there speechless bent and kissed your hand.

1923

ADMONITION

Lock your bedroom doors with terror.
Comb your hair between two lights.
In the gold Venetian chamber
But for them let all be sombre.
Sit! and see reflected lights
Color time within your mirror.

Comb, comb, your bright hair. Rain
Fiery threads upon a shadow.
Stare until you see dilated
Eyes stare out as once the excited
Young men, coming out of shadow,
Stared into a burning pain.

Find the loveliest shroud you own.
Stilt a ceremonious
Height on gilded heels. Then summon
To a rarity grown common
Starved arachnid, the dead-louse
And whatever feeds on bone.

1923

NIGHT

I stand indolently staring at the night
And the stars couched in interminable silences
And have no more comfort of the sight
Than if I had stared at stony images.

They seem so old in their golden disarray—
Bearded with light, nodding in somnolence—
And yet each wheels in a clamorous day
And the turning of young suns is a turbulence.

26

There is no peace whatever we may think:
Even when they have come to decay, like this dry
And rotted moon, even then they cannot slink
Away to a cave like a sick beast, and die.

Propped in their armor they ride the accustomed course;
Like that old king who, when dead and sepulchred,
Was hideously exhumed and set upon his warhorse,
They ride still to the battle, pale and disinterred.

O, let me hood my eyes from this mad night!
The thoughts it calls up are too desolate
For one already in distaste with the fight
From which at least we are borne when our wounds
      are desperate.

1933

TO HIS LATE MISTRESS

Lady, I've not forgot your favors
Though they with others are confused:
Your body's delicate fine savor's
Not lost, but overlaid is
With a later taste of ladies
Who, like you, have not refused.

The desire I had was not spurious:
Rather a young and untried prince
Upstanding in bright armor, furious
In plumes before his war tent—
(When was the cause of wars important?)
But that, Lady, was long since.

I could have sworn he had outlasted
All accidents of fight, long sieges, yes,

Proved against softness when he'd tasted
Completest victory. So he was—
No Hamlet, but young Fortinbras
Whose dying speech was *Nevertheless!*

It was not, then, that you accorded
A common beauty; or that you gave
Ever with a slow and sordid
Hand (that avarice apart
That made you meagre with your heart)
Yet Fortinbras is in his grave.

1933

EPIGRAM

Expert in excess
young Borodine could delight
through nineteen hours, and then,
still please by his conversation.

Fortunate youth! But most
Unfortunate in middle age
Though wit survived when sensuality had ceased.
His final mot: It is not
That the flesh fails, but that
The spirit is appeased.

1933

OCTOBER TRAGEDY

In the woods above Elbeuf, on a mild morning,
M. Phillipoteau, seeker after mushrooms, wandered
With a wicker basket.
                    Dead leaves:
And from white fungi odors of corruption.

May, June (monsieur mused)
As late as August, these woods are used
And the leaves hide under the wall
The boys contorting the turned wrist
The girls crying before they fall.
At the first frost they are not missed
(Autumn's the time for gastronomes)
Who seek at night for furnished rooms.

But now, close to the old wall, on swollen
And gouty feet, bolets—brown mushrooms
Of autumn, scattered on damps.

Autumnal Phillipoteau

Excellent employe, on an
Unemployed morning,

             on brown sodden leaves
Seeks esculent rumps

            follows the old wall
Finding under sagging branches
A corpse blackening. A girl's face. It is late
October. The thickets want privacy.
The police are prompt to memory
(As a minor poet)—A factory girl is missing
The little Lemoine, lost,
Not seen since summer—

           In the July noon
She came to the foreman:

           I must leave at four
I have no choice. I must leave early.

And at four left—

          Where are you going?
Leave me alone! I'll not say
Where I am going.

         Left on a bicycle,
Handbag and lunchbag, strapped to the handlebars.

At nightfall she came home. Her mother
Was disquieted. *What is it? You
Are not the same. You are changed. For months now
I have seen it. What is it?*
                         Leave me alone.

And the next morning left on a bicycle,
Wearing a beret, lunchbag and handbag
Swung from the handlebars.

                         They waited for her
At nightfall. All
Night they waited. She did not come. *She will
Come,* said her mother. *I know she will come.*

In the notebook as when last seen:
In the notebook as on dead leaves:
Brown shawl over pink waist;
Blue skirt, striped; blue shoes—
But the face rotten—Under the old wall,
All overgrown, a shelter.

Charming forest and favorable to loves!
There in April, in hollows,
In the rainlit season, where spring violets
Relinquish their sweet odors and virgins
On dead beds dispose their precious nights,
Morels appear! White-footed mushrooms
Tread the brown leaves, after rain.

                         Remember
Polyphagous Phillipoteau! Autumn has come—

The police are pure in imagination
(As an old pandar to the provincial stage)
Before this putrefaction

They place the lover—
A barely of age and scared butcher's boy.

In the beginning of the afternoon
Under the falling leaves, the rain of chestnuts,
Came M. de Blagny, *juge d'instruction* at Rouen,
M. de Verne, *substitut du procureur de la République*
M. Herriot, *greffier*, accompanied by the doctor Bonvoisin
Neighbor to the defunct, who advanced the opinion
Decomposition being advanced, that autopsy was doubtful.
Silent in derby hats and decent black,
Substantial servants of invisible law,
They stand and wait:
With eyes of wistful weasels wait to hear
A bitter tale of love
And violations on a summer night—
The unwilling struggle and the willing fall.
They wait, themselves exciting
The hot importunate hands that cannot wait
And having failed
To force an opening of the knees, must try
A slight pressure—the lapse from sight, the dark
Breathing, from one throat only—the slow withdrawal
To the feet—the girl not rising.

                    Yes
He said, *It happened here. Four years ago.*
It happened first in these woods here, when I
Was seventeen.

The young man assumed no grief.
Affianced to a corpse he stood
And pulled his cap down. A cigarette
Almost extinct, from his lips
Blackened.

31

You knew

> He could not think
What sum it made, fourteen and seventeen,

> *she was with child?*

On summer nights—

> *I'd heard it. Not from her.*

May, June, as late as August, these woods
Are used. He could not think

> *You'd heard it?*

*I knew. I'm not surprised. For two years now
She's futtered everything in sight.*

> Nothing.

Indignant at indifference, the magistrate
Removes his hat. If love
Cannot last, lust not devise
Remorse when brought
Where the sweet, young and once ecstatic body
Lies in dissolution—Sternly he remands
The young man for a prison audit. Puts on
His hat. The rat
Perceives the weasel eyes. Darkness
Rises from the ground.

Lift this sorry relic of
Boy's desire and girl's love—
It is a repulsive thing!

32

Dark corruption's here begun
Before its hiding from the sun—
Hurry then its burying!

This should not be counted crime:
Love cannot outlast its time.
Find when rainlit April's over
On rotted earth one daffodil,
On leaves, one crocus yellow still,
Then without desire a lover.

Love is lust and an illusion—
Sighings, touchings and confusion
Of sweet bodies, both alive.
Here's no love. Here there lie
Death and dread fecundity
Whose worms on living lovers thrive.

In the meanwhile, the bicycle has been found
Strangely unrusted, returned to the woods—
Its identity destroyed. And the next day
M. Pallet, secretary to the commissariat,
Came to explore the ground
With the passion of an archaeologist
Sifting Pompeii in a sieve. Patiently he found
The buried handbag, emptied; buried
Under leaves, lipstick and pocketglass, the mildewed
Lunchbag of imitation leather; found
A torn blue beret and a packet of letters
Pillaged by the rats, erased by rain;
Found where the corpse had been a silken scarf
And the girl's drawers, maculate with blood;
A napkin four times folded and quite clean;
Found in an old stump,
Thrust out of sight, a folded newspaper

33

Showing the stock quotations for July 29th,
And spots of blood; last a hatpin—
A long thin, sticking hatpin in a mold of leaves.

The police are nothing if not ingenious:
With the celerity of a geometer leaping
Surely to a slow Euclidean fall,
Pallet, pricking his finger,
Vaults on a hatpin, abandoning rape
To fall on abortion. In the woods
Sinister instrument: unsuccessful
The practitioner prefers murder
To disclosure; leaves the corpse
To be discovered by October. Miserable
Conclusion to the kisses of fourteen
To seventeen!

            Then the leaves hid, and the old wall
Gave shelter—Not remembered! But who
When frost is gray upon bitten grassblades
Remembers green? The sun is in Scorpion,
And night's ghost is seen
Walking before the hour of night is come.
Who? Not Blagny, for whom
Winter scratches cold hair? A butcher's boy
Of twenty told that tomorrow
Or after tomorrow he will be free? Excellent
Phillipoteau? Host to Phillipoteau,
He dines on cèpes à la Bordelaise, washes
His memory with red earthy wines, purges
His mind with pungent garlic. The girl's mother
For the last time repeating, She kept alone
She would not eat, and Sometimes softly
Opening the door upon her room, I found
Her weeping—? No one. Unless the unknown

In the dark meditating a hatpin
And a dead mold of leaves perhaps remembers.
1933

ACCOUNT OF A CRIME

Irritable at wires, in his cage
The green parrot screamed. But most his fears
Harassed him: middle age
And the poor mediocrity of his sort
The banter of the breakfast table
And as he thought the endlessness of life.
At last one morning broke
The mainspring of his watch. Then he knew
His hour at last. And silencing his wife
With a loud pistol he saw the smoke
Drift slowly toward the breakfast table.
And still behind its wires that most execrable
Green thing clawed and shrilled. He waited the report
More than the wound, when with shut eyes he drew
And shot away his life. His dying ears
Heard on its wires the parrot's irritable rage.

1933

ENCOUNTER

In the rags of a wind
A man who was proud
Called out to me, Wait!
The low light was late
When he came: I have sinned
And must say it aloud!

35

Together we walked;
The late light was yellow
On the inland marsh,
Cold yellow and harsh
Where cattails stalked
And salt grass was sallow.

I heard his heart beat
Between each word.
What he said was this:
I have given a kiss
As Iscariot's sweet
When he hurt Our Lord.

He was done and a silence
Came down on my stare.
His eyes were dark O's
And a great bird rose
Through the tarnished air
Of those sluggish islands.

He lifted a face
Which crowned thorns had bled.
But I said nothing
Of my great loathing
And for my embrace
He held his head.

He had no shame:
I heard the blood drip
Through the white rib bone
Of his skeleton.
And I stood with cold lip
Whose sin was the same.

1933

MARTYR'S HILL

And in this street
Dawn begins not as light
But as the sound of ashmen's feet
And the young man passes doors
That have the odor of sleep

Down a descending
Perspective of gray houses.
If this is day it has
The complexion of a night-beggar's
Unshaven and disastrous face.
Down the paved hill
He goes, unsteadily, as though
He went to a precipice.

The little whores have all gone in
And gray as mice
Creep to some hole stuffed against today.
Old newspapers are illegible yesterdays.
None can now believe in sin
But he now believes in vice.

The taxis roll before the Trinity
The taxis roll about the empty square
Like billiard balls in a room one has left.
At the corner of Saint Lazarus
Workmen lean on coffee cups
Devouring crescents. Blouses
Bluer than the sky and as the morning ravenous.

He seems to smoke a cigarette.
And leaning on a bar of zinc
The tired lover tries to think.

Memory wipes away the night
As a damp rag might smear a dirty glass.
Above the bar he sees another face.

1933

ALIENS

When snow
Stays in the street on garbage cans
There are those who when night is tired
Relinquish silence in unheated rooms.
I've stood upon their roofs. I have seen
The moon above their watertowers. They only know
Winter by this snow.

There is a snow
Which does not fall from heaven
Nor melt into the earth,
And theirs it is, who have no heaven
And have abandoned the back-laboring earth.
They have no silence, for their snow
Falls to a sound of grinding brakes and gears
Of trains that run through darkness and through snow.
They have no silence and they have no tears.

They have no silence and they have no love.
They sit about their nothingness
As men from habit sit by empty stoves.
They only say, Things might be worse,
For whom Time waits
As a hearse waits by a tenement door.
They have no silence as they have no years.
Only by starts their minds gape awfully,
Dark as cellars where Italian boys
Harass the tropics to the subway's roar.

It is the retirement of the sun
That leaves these garbage cans in snow.
Winter is motion. The direction
Is not known whither all these planets go.

1933

AN ENGLISH LADY

1922

In a small most Viennese hotel, she sits,
A lady, diminutive among the Baedekers.
Last year she traversed Spain with a courier
And saw Cordoba of the Moors and Saint James of Compostella.
This year she tours the Tyrol second class
With a handbag bought in Regent Street
And a secondhand umbrella.
Her hat is not what it was at all.
Her pince-nez pauses on the point to fall.
Her waterproof in covering her reveals the English soul.
Once she spent two years in London
With a cousin of Colonel Condom's
Just to do the art museums and the lesser galleries;
Especially she admired Sir Laurence Alma-Tadema
And the great Sir Thomas Lawrence. Next winter
She will spend in Florence
In a pension near the Pitti Palace.
She is long past the changes of the moon.
You may yet find her African
Exploring forums with a pious spade
Or wrapped in veils against the desert sand
Pursuing nothing but a nothing that shall sound
With the gold and amorous anger
Of laughing Antony in his Herculean armor.

39

Remembering Lady Hester Stanhope in her retirement
One bows in envious silence toward the British Islands.
1933

CHÂTEAU À VENDRE

The old château is pink and gray:
The rich façade is painted plaster.
There the Americans have installed
Copper heat and all
The conveniences of modern cold
And bathtubs where dolphins' mouths
Spout water with an antique finish.
They've also had to fortify the walls.

Winter includes the parc
A wilderness of indistinguishable twigs
And alleys leading
To a leaden nebula, from which
The trees emerge distinctly French.

The sun looks toward England
With the old, blind, civilized smile
Of Madame du Deffand
On Horace Walpole.

1931

RIVIERA

When like the sun retired southward

The Duchess arrived at Cannes
With rugs, trunks, hairless Mexican dogs
And two blond harried maids

The manager of the Palace Hotel
Came through that air
Like a long afternoon in a dusty conservatory
And down the almost marble stair
A little wearily
                    to meet her

She met him
                    with a massive countenance
Like a well-rouged stone.
                                        Sprawled
Under the palm trees, idle
As a native, smoking
Through one funnel of a tug
Blue the Mediterranean lay.

                                        Clapped
His hands, the cut-away

                                        Whereupon
Aroused,
                    the sudden and obsequious sea
Sharply advanced, wave after wave,
Innumerably bowing,
                              curled
And powdered flunkeys
                                   And the Duchess
With a step and a smile allowed
(Both enormous) the usual reception
Pages porters maids
                              herself
To proceed

1933

41

THE RETURN

Night and we heard heavy and cadenced hoofbeats
Of troops departing: the last cohorts left
By the North Gate. That night some listened late
Leaning their eyelids toward Septentrion.

Morning flared and the young tore down the trophies
And warring ornaments: arches were strong
And in the sun but stone; no longer conquests
Circled our columns; all our state was down

In fragments. In the dust, old men with tufted
Eyebrows whiter than sunbaked faces gulped
As it fell. But they no more than we remembered
The old sea-fights, the soldiers' names and sculptors'.

We did not know the end was coming: nor why
It came; only that long before the end
Were many wanted to die. Then vultures starved
And sailed more slowly in the sky.

We still had taxes. Salt was high. The soldiers
Gone. Now there was much drinking and lewd
Houses all night loud with riot. But only
For a time. Soon the taverns had no roofs.

Strangely it was the young the almost boys
Who first abandoned hope; the old still lived
A little, at last a little lived in eyes.
It was the young whose child did not survive.

Some slept beneath the simulacra, until
The gods' faces froze. Then was fear.
Some had response in dreams, but morning restored
Interrogation. Then O then, O ruins!

42

Temples of Neptune invaded by the sea
And dolphins streaked like streams sportive
As sunlight rode and over the rushing floors
The sea unfurled and what was blue raced silver.

1933

BALLET

Upon the walls

Horses of Chirico with crinkled locks
Trotted obedient to

Sculptured youths

In silence stood, confused

and opened doors

while

Through the window leaned (the dark was dark behind)
Viscera and cerebral desires.

And Archaeologists announced

(Voices portentous as those heard in dreams)
Vast cities of Atlantis discovered in a skull
Columns and forums, forms of eyeless gods

A rout of dancers then came in:

Dancers who were young in dances that were dead.

And while they danced

Goddesses sat

In squat armchairs and from their awful laps
Disclosed a Roman débris

shafts of stone

Serene and blind

The old men danced

Their high hats walled in brick, while through their beards

Rustled the seashells and the waves
                              the waves
That sometime smiled in wrinkled bliss
Around the margins of the morning world.

1933

HUNGER AND THIRST

Shrieks in dark leaves. The rumpled owl
Disgorges undigested bones
And feathered bits of lesser fowl.

When black obese flies are few
Starved spiders have been seen to drink
Gold mornings in a round of dew.

The charlatan beneath his tent
With a wide flourish of hand
Consumes a fiery element.

There have been soldiers, too, who drank
A yellow water from steel casques
Not minding how the sunlight stank.

And some have fed on air that sang
From skulls where under hollow darks
Dust sneered to show a horny fang.

And Ugolino's horrible hunger
We too have known, and known too well,
The strength that stretches famine longer.

We too have known within our cell
Voices entreat us that we feed
On flesh whose bone we loved too well.

1932

BEHAVIOR OF THE SUN

The wasps had reproduced Pompeii
Excavating palaces from ashes.
My cousin pointed the way
And the sunlight came in flashes.

Sir John Harrington was not known
As the architect of that outhouse.
Sir Thomas Urquart, in the bone,
Cast his shadow upon us.

Spiders with the insistence of pedants
Had recovered whole mythologies.
When instructed in the dance
Pan's beat was louder than Mercury's.

The dials pointed to twelves
Though the clock towers struck but One.
Thus being left to ourselves
We altered the height of the sun.

He conjugated Pretend
In the strict interests of science.
I being but ten could lend
Only an interested compliance.

The wasps had reproduced Pompeii
Excavating palaces from ashes.
My cousin pointed the way.
Meanwhile the sun came in flashes.

1933

BEYOND CONNECTICUT, BEYOND THE SEA

When I look into my sons' eyes I see
The color of seawater, blue
Under cold shores. Their bodies will be tall.
Their hair has come to them from far off,
Washing like seaweed through diverse waters.

Tall with fair hair, they lived in islands
Who long had lived
Ravaging the shores: swords that arrived
Upon the rising wave
Slowly. Always they came westward.
Their stranded keels were sure in the sand.

(But back of bronze is stone, beyond the seamists
Is the silence of old lands and grave shards
Savage and then no longer human secrets.)

They came to the sea-isles. Beyond the sea
The silence of peninsulas of snow. I take
My name and blood from a poor boy
Stolen in the islands, whipped at sea,
And sold to a Connecticut farmer.

Eleazar Bishop lived to be old; he died
When old, still stooping over stones
That had come with Bethia, his wife. Dead
They dug him shallow and covered him over
With a clatter of stones from the uncleared hillside.

He left behind him tall seven sons.
Another Eleazar straddled stones
And did not find them fertile.

Thomas Bishop
Was bulleted by the British
In his revolutionary buttocks, climbing
A railfence at Breed's Hill.

Isaac Bishop strode upon a continent
And old still stared, at seventy years
Insatiable, upon the setting sun.

And John Bishop wandered south
When long war had burned the corn
And saw his sons stoned, little boys.

And Jonathan Bishop first aspired
To make that landscape desolate
In pigments black and green and white.

These are my bones, my bones that lie
Six skeletons underground
And clayed in ruin
On their hillsides keep,
As winds are held in autumn rusted leaves,
Aging their rustic names.

This is my blood, my blood that beats
In blithe boys' bodies
And shall yet run (O death!)
Upon a bright inhabited star.

But more there are that lie
'Neath snows more northern than Connecticut
Or round the sea-isles drift, dissolved
To salt and drowned, dead bones that rise upon the surf
And prompt the sea to whispers.

1933

MY GRANDFATHER KEPT PEACOCKS

When other reasons for pride were gone
Winters he sat by the green-primed woodbox
And pine-knots flared upon a meditation
Of wild blue eyes and a grey beard stalked
On the thin despair of a dwindling hand.
Frost had been kind: windows gave back
A glazed white stare of crazy eyes but blind.
Carpets were windy stripes upon the floor.
The kitchen planks were wide and scoured with sand.
He could not see unless he undertook the door
Those arrogant birds, whom the wind balked
In their poor progress through the snow.
He could not touch the door; he did not dare
Because of a looking glass beside the door.
He would not risk the smallest crack
Of snow, lest death should see him there
Looking from out the glass beside the door.

1933

THIS DIM AND PTOLEMAIC MAN

For forty years, for forty-one,
Sparing the profits of the sun,
This farmer piled his meagre hoard
To buy at last a rattly Ford.

Now crouched on a scared smile he feels
Motion spurt beneath his heels,
Rheumatically intent shifts gears,
Unloosens joints of rustic years.

Morning light obscures the stars,
He swerves avoiding other cars,
Wheels with the road, does not discern
He eastward goes at every turn,

Nor how his aged limbs are hurled
Through all the motions of the world,
How wild past farms, past ricks, past trees,
He perishes toward Hercules.

1933

THE ANCESTORS

The house leaks and leans. Night's roof-timbers glut
   To rain on those wide planks the dead have thinned
With their loud feet. Here where the door is shut
   We sit to shudder in the rising wind.

A great bed in the chamber off the hall
   Whispers its curtains. White its counterpane
And white the faces that have lain there, all
   Corrupt in silence, noble, skulled by rain.

Why should the wind rise now? It never rose
   Like this before! Where will the worse than poor
Porch their unsheltered beards and pierce their clothes
   This night with rain? Where persecute their store

Of pitiless lice? Where sleep? On nights like these
   Whose spacious wars living and dead exhume
What calm to send the mind on the stone ease
   Of passions ruining in the sculptured tomb!

1933

PERSPECTIVES ARE PRECIPICES

Sister Anne, Sister Anne,
Do you see anybody coming?

   I see a distance of black yews
   Long as the history of the Jews.

I see a road sunned with white sand,
Wide plains surrounding silence. And

Far-off, a broken colonnade
That overthrows the sun with shade.

Sister Anne, Sister Anne,
Do you see nobody coming?

           A man

Upon that road a man who goes
Dragging a shadow by its toes.

Diminishing he goes, head bare
Of any covering even hair.

A pitcher depending from one hand
Goes mouth down. And dry is sand

Sister Anne, Sister Anne,
What do you see?

       His dwindling stride. And he seems blind
       Or worse to the prone man behind.

Sister Anne! Sister Anne!

       I see a road. Beyond nowhere
       Defined by cirrus and blue air.

       I saw a man but he is gone
       His shadow gone into the sun.

1933

MINUTE PARTICULARS

1935

MINUTE PARTICULARS

O LET NOT VIRTUE SEEK

Above these continents and inconstant shores!

The morning sands concede their contours
To the sea.
        Aspire to wings! The mountain towns
Soon lose their towers.

           Curving the wind's wild bank
Assault with upward surge the uncalm dream:

In uncompanionable blue lust of air
Spiral in steel, assume an Icarian light
And ever circling ever toward go
The astounding sun
          that burning blest
Vehement constancy of ever fire.

             And past
Curriculums of summer cloud, shine over us
(If eyes can strain so far)
Curvetting silver wings.

        Soar O vast!
Where no breath survives
         And slowly into
The deepening day of Cytherean blue, scale
Atomy!

There breathe and there exult,
Cirrus an exhalation far below,
                                        a white
A nothing
                and look down
                                        the Alps giddily
Lost, white points of snow; remote shores.

Let drone your engines, drop, and dreadfully
Down discern
                Italy subject to two seas
And once more rise (who still must move and can
No more poise than can the únmortal moon)
The deepening vault of violet
Venture
                and look down
                                        dark Adriatic
In a surf of cloud and in the wing's wired turn
Imagined azure gulfed by the Genoese.

Nor only look upon those promontories
And those shores!
                        But once again wheel
And guard the sun, daring and descending, stare
Upon that height
                        unattainable

                                        —*E pur si muove*

It is for you to tell us
                        Astronomers

In the midst of living suns we are
Spun toward death—the earth a star among
Other stars

54

You spend your nights in distance
And your stir of silence
Is infinitely gilded!

But so small
Only under your eyelids have you seen us
                              Sphere
Which death distinguishes, star whose surface
Starts an animal that keeps its dead, whose crust
Was cooled to corrupt in tombs

                         You have seen much
Since first, chilled by the night-dews, patient
On stilly terraces, you stood and in an amaze
Of glitter monstered the heavens. You have learned much,
Historian of undying dynasties,
In a long patience.

                         And now adventurous
You sit and with thin wires, at night,
Measure Andromeda. Laboriously
Twiddling screws you twist your neck, adjust
Your sights, and squint:
                         A foam of light
Breaks on the glass
                         destroys a wave
Whose crest was lifted farther than
The young Aeneas when he wrung
His boy's wet hair and on the sea-rock wept,
Naked, longing for war.
                         Increase your sums,
Musician of numbers! You increase
The speculation of our eyes.
                         You have given us
Space
        until we die of a surfeit of stars

Once we were dead at seventy years
And tired were laid with white hairs in the ground.
Now we are young and rot with a million years.

Pedant of motion!
                    In ephemerides
You note a moment, in the plunge, a moment
Only true, of suns, golden Actaeons
Pursued by revolving splendors, hounds in blind
Circles panting, biding their prey. Time? What shall
We do with time? You have given us unavailable
Millenniums and we stifle for a second
When desire bends our knees above our love. Time?
What shall we do with time? Your hours are run
On glorious glasses, through which deserts spill
And noon is still unsanded. You have given us
Time. We have time. Time!
I do not know. Some say that you have taken away
More than Proserpine lost when she lost the spring.

But you, dusting the dandruff from your collar, call
And whistle to those stars whose blind and backward glare
Goes over the cliff of time and down
And down
Where nothing is an empty wind.

And now come down, steel carapaces,
Ambitious and undisastrous sons of the Sun,
Come down. And you, old men, astronomers
With your tempestuous modesty, come
With instruments and bring your quadrants
(Which you'll need). This is another task. Now take
The height and shadow of our man, our noble
Coriolanus, who still armors the earth,
Albeit dead and never but a man,

And tell us once again what stature his
And what his stride, who nothing asked
Even of a god but his eternity!

1935

A DEFENSE

I would not interdict
Unscrupulous passion.
But the cloud is not strict
In its shape as the sun
For a cloud cannot win
To a sun's discipline.

We have seen states
Scatter and saints go down.
The storm abates
Destruction goes on
And only the wind exults
In the storm's results.

I would ask of the proud
They protect their lust.
For lowering could
And rising dust,
These go. Our pain
Is great, but we remain.

Fools of the intellect
And the starved bone
Were content to erect
Their rage upon
These disasters of blood.
But can they carve in mud?

We bide this storm
In naked emptiness
And find no wandering warm
To the night's distress.
By the gleam of stable straw
I stone one thought as law.

1934

THE MOTHERS

Sealights reflected on the rocks
And sunlight baffled by the waves:

O shores! what greens there are that waver in the shallows,
What depths of being, invading blues,
What shadows under waves!

They sit like vast shadows on the rocks.
They stand and are women on the sands.
Their hands are sober on the rocks
And in their eyes are myths conceived.

These hands have dug, these loins have labored,
These eyes have seen
The man that leaned above them, hasty,
They have known the hands that pushed their thighs apart.
The ecstasy they have known and the burning,
The heart against the heart
The ecstasy they have known and the burden,
The heart under the heart.
Then the child's hand that gropes across the heart.

But now they sit by the seas
And are unmoved by the lisping sands
Or by the losing splendor of the shelly moon.

Our course, I think, is nearer to the sun.
Over their eyelids, in ethereal bronze
Deploy, Icarus! For among their rocks
Are depths where a man might drown.

What shall we do? We are their sons,
Insane of courage, lost to will,
Failing, not fathers to our sons—

Serene, in the ears of the flesh, they hear
The rude white-flashing rock-noise.
Their seas have not the fret of fortune,
In our appeasement is their peace.

When they set out upon these sands
It will be, huge feet, toward eternity.
With the calm march of night they will go
And toward the assuagement of goddesses.

In what regions, by what shores,
White marts and towers,
By what margins of what noisier seas,
Do I think thee to be, my country?

After revolt, what triumph and what deaths?
1934

APPARITION

I have seen in the Virginia forest
Cool pallid light of an undersea day;
Coral of the isles arose, encrusted spray,
Branches submerged and overhead wild shell.

59

What was it then I saw? Flashing sea-scale,
Flicker of tail? Sea-bud, sunlight or syren
Smiling, which even in a boy might move
Felicity, or failing scatter foam as hail?

What did I then? Rose, swam or sank.
The end was moss. Around me April chuckled,
The catbird cried upon a dogwood bough,
And day came crashing through pale judas-bud.

1935

COUNSEL OF GRIEF

Assume your dignity
Among forgotten tombs!
Now that the mind assumes
Thoughtlessness of despair,
And crazed our eyeballs stare
As ancient statues who,
Once apparelled in light,
Untoppled amid columns
Falling, stood and unmoved
Saw in the shards below
Smoke the throats of their sons—
Into your unloved night
Accept this elegy.
This is the son you loved.

You had drawn such content
From the sweet dugs of earth,
That living, you never refused
The lavish outlay of the sun.
How then will you consent,
Being dead to that dearth
With which the dead are used?

O how will you consent,
Whose love was luminous
As though already won
Its immortality?
That light was shed on us.
Only of love were you proud.
That pride is broken at last,
Too poor you are for the cost
In the impoverished shroud.

Assume your dignity,
And in that silence
Beyond experience
Of all our loneliness,
Smile! It is a lonely
Mirth the dead have.
But theirs is the only
Smile risks never to be less
Whose fortune is the grave.

1935

ANOTHER ACTAEON

I have come here fleeing I know not what
Fate. I know not what I fled from
Then in the moonlight, in the glass-gray air
Running in moonlight, in the gray light
Of grass-wet air. Then in the thickets I heard them
Scattering light feet, running, spattering
Leaves and crashing—as though they were hunting—
Branches. Naked shadows. Pulsating hoofbeats.
But the thickets dark. There was seen
Neither horn, nor uprearing haunches, nor even
The long low lope of a hound crossing the glade
And leaping with deep teeth into a neck.

It may be it was not a death I heard there.
But here where I have come, to die,
Or merely not to die, is the only question.
What have I fled from? What do I ask for?
I wake to my shame and the wood is lonely.

1935

SOUTHERN PINES

White pine, yellow pine,
The first man fearing the forest
Felled trees, afraid of shadow,
His own shade in the shadow of pinewoods.

Slash pine, loblolly,
The second man wore tarheels,
Slashed pine, gashed pine,
The silent land changed to a sea-charge.

Short leaf, long leaf,
The third man had aching pockets.
Mill town, lumber mill,
And buzzards sailed the piney barrens.

Cut pine, burnt pine,
The fourth man's eyes burned in starvation.
Bone-back cattle, razor-back hogs
Achieve the seedling, end the pinewoods.

1935

NIGHT AND DAY

I

Heavy with haze
By old back fences
Stunted and torn

Hunted and starved
By hunger upborne
The carrion women
The crow-back men
Pick civilization
From garbage cans.

From syphilitic doorways
Spectres appear
Streets of failure
Each face a fear
Bodies crushed
Boys and girls
Between rail and wall
In darkened doorways
And unlit halls.

II

Apparitions of precision
Pressed by shadows
To supremacy in speed:
Servers made servile
Supine in pride
Paced by machines:
Racing abstractions
Marvellously making
Pretense of plenty:

And the end what?
More speed, more hunger.

1936

AN INTERLUDE

Our indolence was despair. We were still at times struck
When morning attained the deiformed emperors

Where they stood, gaudy in armor, with laurels crowned,
One arm uplifted among the columns.

                                        There was never
Of course, any lack of statues to instruct us
In the aspect of virtue: magnanimous brows
Sterner than marble; in the sun's silence
Aquiline stares.

                        Yet it was trying to behold
Depravity in the guards: propped as soldiers
By the gates, a few old seasoned cutthroats
With limping reputations; handsome and husky goatherds,
Culled from the border hills, paid for and pampered
Out of our taxes; boys naughty as goats,
No wounds but in nerves, who nightly extolled
Their vices by Hadrian's monument and in broad day
Bartered equipment by the shaft of light
Where Victory wings the square.
                                        They jeered
Seeing the disorder, dust, stains, lagging wounds
Of the retreating army
                        (The first in our annals—
What eyes the windows wore!)
                                        They clambered to jeer.

The Emperor arrived at midnight, complaining
Discreetly of the discipline. He must wait,
He said, opportunity
To retrieve both his own
And the nation's glory. Still on horseback,
He did not fail to recall our former fortunes;
Unbuckling swore at his orderly;
Summoned the generals
And for an hour harangued them in his tent:

Passes over the mountains could be entrusted
Only to troops of approvèd valor. Guards must be posted
Along all thoroughfares, doubled on crossroad,
With orders, and swords, to soothe this demented
Uproar and fear of the populace.

                                        Deliberate
Even in the worst disease of his defeat,
The infecting tumult, he found time
Before morning to consult with others
On their causes for our long decline from greatness.
It was his opinion, he had long thought
And was more than ever convinced, nothing
Could be done for the army, nothing would again
Incite its ardor, unless manners were brought back
To their former glorious severity. No health else
In the state. Therefore, he proposed,
At the earliest possible moment, to revive
The long obsolete office of censor.

                                        Revenue
Would have to be increased, but without, he insisted,
Adding to the already crushing burden of the wealthy.
The populace was to be separate once more as a class.
The hungry would be fed, of course, but the mob
Would have to curb its rage for riots. To prevent
These continual manifestations of envy, spite
And misery, he hereby restored
The equestrian order to all its rank and privileges.

Something, to be sure, would have to be done
For the peasantry, something, he was not sure,
But something, he supposed, along the lines of Augustus.
He would supply the army with all the needed statistics.
What might have come of all this we shall never know.

For nothing came of it, beyond some compilations of distress
Before the battle of the bogs.

                    Our undoing, it seems,
Was the blenching and scattered retreat of the swift barbarians.
Starved, for the countryside was exhausted, they did not refuse
Battle, but on the touch of our armies broke and fled,
Some without weapons. The Emperor, desiring to strike terror,
In haste pursued them with harassing swords
Beyond the third line, across salt meadows,
Into the marshes.

His body was never recovered. Here fortune turned.
All was adverse to our arms. The marsh, thick with ooze,
Sinking under those who fought, their armor weighted and the
        water deep.
Nor could they wield, in that morass, our heavy javelins.

We have heard the new Emperor proclaims
Our immediate deliverance. Medals have been struck off
Portraying him as Hercules the Victor
And as Mars the Avenger.

In the meantime, the barbarians are back in the passes.
Nothing is left but to stay devastation by tribute.
1936

NO MORE THE SENATOR

To put off the insignia,
The gold-laced cothurnus, to lay aside
The honors of an office that had long been futile,
Was not hard. Nor was it severe,
Not at my age, to close the doors upon the Capitol,
To say, I have looked upon these statues for the last time.

For the Caesars have long been extinct: the eyebrows
Concise upon seeing eyes and the whole face
Stern upon conquest. I have seen them only in stone.
                    The name
Snatched up by barbarians and worn with a swagger
Is on bearded faces and a burst of vacant eyeballs.

It is so long we have known our divinities only through Ovid
And mentioned their names only on official occasions.

It was not hard. With my charge of years
I wear chastity as quietly as I wear
White hairs. I have not found it hard
This custom of beans, coarse bread, cold water
And a bed that shortens nights. Once in a while
I long for quail. But that's not much. It is
The conduct of the mind that's hard to change.

How shall I approach the Virgin, lowly,
Enthroned in the dim blue, when the enamored stars
Crowning increase their splendor? How shall I believe
When I have lost all custom of belief?
The slaves here have an advantage. For them
It is a vain ambition to discern
The variousness of God the Father God the Son God the
                    Immanent and Most Holy Ghost.
As well ask yellow trumpets to distinguish
The subtleties of one from another silence
When all they ask is they may blow again!

It is not a dispute within the doctrine
Can dislodge me. I have conceived with the mind
And am convinced in the mind—thanks that my father
As a boy put me always to the best
Rhetoricians! No. And not to think
Where thinking cannot alter understanding

Is perhaps wise. I have no doubts. And still
I say, Suppose there is a doubt—suppose
Our fathers were not fools!

My faith in God is consoled by a cell.
But outside is the long dusty road and soldiers riding,
Rising with that trick of stirrups learned in the North.
And summer dusts the olive trees
And crows fly silver winging into the sun
And along the road, under the pines, those other stones,
Coffers filled with slower dust, Roman, dropped from bones.

I am convinced that God will raise me from the dead.
But dying and not dead, old in a body
That was once loved, I cannot change
The custom of my mind. So I have set
These monks over whom God hung me like a whip
To multiplying manuscripts. For God, they say,
So loved the world . . . I know, I say,
The whole world . . . That the whole world. . . . But these
He did not save. Christ did not die for poets.
So I say Hurry!
    Hurry the Clouds!
        For heaven is high
And cannot hear our comedies. Hurry
My Seneca and Euripides!
       For tragedy stays here.

We'll keep no fasts if fasting blurs your eyes.
Whatever else is lost, O them
Whom God did not, Caesar will not, slaves cannot,
Save! For I am old. And I have seen
The crows feed black when gathered to the grain.
They also die: poets
Whose immortality grows by the river bed in reeds.

1935

NEW ENGLAND

I. Return to Connecticut

Fall, and we came to the rock-bleached pasture;
Straggled by cedars, the rocks remain.
Scarlet disasters, sweet-gum and sumach,
Sank without wind. What was there left?

Homeless we wandered. A black-tailed grackle
Vilely eyed us. Hunger on a fence-rail,
His way was southward. I had returned
To the home of my fathers. Dishonored houses,

Decaying farmlands. I had returned
To the land of my fathers without their courage,
Without their hope. Without their faith,
I had returned to the land of my fathers.

What was there left of me, living, but winter,
A borrowed dwelling, a long season
Of straggling cedars in black procession,
Bowed as when burials are blest in rain?

1936

II. Moving Landscape with Falling Rain

Woodlands are lost upon a haze
Of hills and overlapping spurs;
A dripping rain of sumach strays
A stony solitude of firs.

A hillside shows its jagged teeth
And white the headstones fall askew.
Winter not passion sleeps beneath
The snowy names of Pettigrew.

69

The wilderness comes to the verge
Of cinders in this chimney'd town,
And snow and Fords and rust-tins merge
In hollows where the rain is brown.

There is no sustenance in this ground
Unless we live on bones or sweat;
In graves the bones. Above are bound
The Lithuanian, Pole and Lett.

Black girders bridge with iron rain
A desolation spreading tracks.
Twilight converts a dwindling train
Into a waste of tin-roof'd shacks,

Tar-paper sides where winter seeps
And soot assures a crust to snow.
The traffic stops, the mind escapes,
But the dead heart stays below.

1936

III. THE WONDERS OF SCIENCE

He squats in Quincy Adams' seat
Dishonorable hulk of hair and bone.
Amazed the planets hear his bleat
Across the spacious microphone.

1936

IV. WINTER PRINT

Snow in Connecticut is thatched
With orange mist and purple weed,
Runneled by rain and rudely patched
By rocks that cannot go to seed.

What cold pursuit those dreams! What suns
Tortured with winds snow-hills like these!
And dark the asphalt river runs
Under the unreflected trees.

1936

V. Season of Wrath

New England was nothing, not even time,
Unless we count the lapse of days a calendar,
Falling of snow and drift of snowbirds winter,
Yellow trout-lilies, green skunk-cabbage, spring.

I was concealed in another year
Concluding an agony of youth
Long dreamt of, once more brought to day,
Compiling passion in disordered words.

Yet the mink fished daily on a slate of ice,
Came daily to the stream, on the rockfence
Played, or appeared to play, for his concern
Was serious. Killing, the chilled mouse knew his tooth.

The newspapers brought reports of strikes: shootings,
Heads broken, or unbandaged led to crime.
Night, unseen snow in woods, the hungry fox
Paused, lifted his paw into the scentless wind.

This was that time, season of crimes and wrath.

1936

A RECOLLECTION

Famously she descended, her red hair
Unbound and bronzed by sea-reflections, caught
Crinkled with sea-pearls. The fine slender taut
Knees that let down her feet upon the air,

71

Young breasts, slim flanks and golden quarries were
Odder than when the young distraught
Unknown Venetian, painting her portrait, thought
He'd not imagined what he painted there.

And I too commerced with that golden cloud:
Lipped her delicious hands and had my ease
Faring fantastically, perversely proud.

All loveliness demands our courtesies.
Since she was dead I praised her as I could
Silently, among the Barberini bees.

1934

THE COMING OF PERSEPHONE

In the April season
When wild young jonquils
Wake in the underwood,
Rivalling anemones
Nimble in the wind,
On leaf-mold with light step,
Shyly approaching
Sunlight, Persephone
Left the shadows,
With breath of morning
Amazing meadows,
Apparent April,
Restored bright air;
Replenishing winds
With sprightly fragrance,
Plucked white sprigs
Of the wild plum's spring;
Darting pursued
Grape-hyacinth and pheasant-eye,

Undying Narcissus
Won from the underworld
Pert from decay;
Pungently gathered
Blue-eyed knot-grass
And staring to eastward
White-starry asphodel;
Demeter's daughter,
Her shoulders shining
With locks all loosely
Showered like morning,
Cooler than love,
But covered with longing,
Brightness beset
With a burden of blossoming,
Girl's bosom half bare
Half golden from clusters,
Divineness displaying
By the thong loosened,
Slender white thighs
Striding from folds,
An earthly daughter,
All dewy descended
Barefoot to shingle,
Unwarily wandered
On sobbing sands,
Pranking with color
Wastes of shell,
And destined bride
Deposed clouds,
On all that seacoast
Assuring an azure
Accession of light.

1936

METAMORPHOSIS

Then when I lay by her side
Was to lie on a hillock of snow;
Had I lain by one that had died
I had not shivered so.
How can this be in love
Only our shudder can know.

I was not cold for I lay
With all the sinews of love
Strung taut for the trying play.
And my hand was strong above
Her hand. And hastening
Our kisses were not enough.

For all that shaking was turned
Into a clearness of fire
That stood still while it burned.
Delay advised desire
And desire cried out at delay
Being cheated of his require.

There was no shame in that
Consuming nakedness,
For we were one; and a disparate
Skin is love's own dress.
But our division of air
Was burned between ecstasies.

With what wild flight I ranged
And never left her breast!
And burdened there was changed
Into a cloud or a beast,
Continual metamorphosis
Into all that is strangest.

But this is not now as it was.
Once we defeated all time.
Sand was stopped in our glass
While centuries ran to their chime.
But this is not now as it was
For all has been changed by time.

What have I done that she
Should take such goodness away?
I go from felicity.
O lovers who now defray
The cost of your heavy limbs,
Know I have had my day!

1934

THE TREE

Return to the tree!
Let the man stand
Radiantly
Let him approach and lean
To boughs of reluctant green.

For a tree must rise
From a hidden root
To the sun-rimmed fruit,
And stalwart thighs
To the shade recall
How a tree grows tall.

And close beside
Let a woman crouch,
Longing to touch,
But the touch denied
Until embraced
By the lips with death's taste.

75

Bring fate to grasp
In the hid leaves
What the hand receives
From a serpent clasp
Of cold coils. Unclose
That green and sinuous repose.

In abashed air
Let him increase
Her comeliness
With a strong stare,
The sun's beat confused
With a beauty unused.

Then a sudden light
Like a bird will skip
From leaf to leaf's tip
Singing, a bright
Burnish of desire
Bordering all their tree with fire.

From the living stem
Such sustenance
Draws into their dance
Stars follow them.
Clasping they control
The coursing light from pole to pole.

Let them fructify
Their tree of death!
With brute breath
Let them die!
All delight of leaf and sun
Dreams of dissolution.

From the forced bough,
Fruit despoiled,
Serpent-coiled,
The end foreknow.
There where all the planets sang
See him a destroyer hang!

1936

YOUR CHASE HAD A BEAST IN VIEW

Long time those gay and spotted hides
We hunted, riding: luxurious
Leopards in the forest slid.
At times it seemed they hunted us.

For just behind green tendrils they,
Seen and unseen, lengthened slunk;
Where the sun groped a greener day
They overleapt the rotted trunk.

And long we rode and still within
The forest eyes. Hidden we felt
A sinewy speed. A javelin
Once lifted to a snarling pelt

And fell and straightened to the hand.
Both knew that death must be delayed,
And on we rode, the leopards and
The followed, following, cavalcade.

O happiness! The lively long
Advancing of each golden beast!
The odor of their might was strong,
The morning wind was in the East.

But noon was cruel on our sight.
We rode into the forest's hem
And when the sun was at its height
In a small glade we slaughtered them.

We cut each throat. We dragged our knives
Across each looking throat. Their blood
Dyed death upon our hands. Our lives
Exultant spurted in the flood,

A moment young. Then silence broke
At the sweet destruction of
Those spotted beasts. And a shout spoke.
The youngest sang a stranger love.

Only in singing it might be
Supported by the sense alone,
One syllable of ecstasy
Confusing shame, confounding bone.

1934

EXPERIENCE IN THE WEST

I. THE BURNING WHEEL

They followed the course of heaven as before
Trojan in smoky armor westward fled
Disastrous walls and on his shoulders bore
A dotard recollection had made mad,

Depraved by years, Anchises: on the strong
Tall bronze upborne, small sack of impotence;
Yet still he wore the look of one who young
Had closed with Love in cloudy radiance.

So the discoverers when they wading came
From shallow ships and climbed the wooded shores:
They saw the west, a sky of falling flame,
And by the streams savage ambassadors.

O happy, brave and vast adventure! Where
Each day the sun beat rivers of new gold;
The wild grape ripened, springs reflected fear;
The wild deer fled; the bright snake danger coiled.

They, too, the stalwart conquerors of space,
Each on his shoulders wore a wise delirium
Of memory and age: ghostly embrace
Of fathers slanted toward a western tomb.

A hundred and a hundred years they stayed
Aloft, until they were as light as autumn
Shells of locusts. Where then were they laid?
And in what wilderness oblivion?

1936

II. GREEN CENTURIES

Courage and hope demand
For here the heart was sound.
The long man strode apart
In green no soul was found,
In that green savage clime
Such ignorance of time.

The green parrot's scream
Clung to the wild-tree fruit.
The wild foot tracked a stream.
What anger could confute
Green crowns of crashing bough
When every day dawned Now?

79

Time dreams eternity.
Their nights were starred with space.
But now an idle frown
Compels the death-set face,
Where dwindled to a glaze
Angers an old hawk's gaze.

1936

III. Loss in the West

Cast out of the fray
The man in the coonskin cap.
His curse is a sneer. He has had his day.

The vile rattle
Remains, the wild pigeon gone and slaughtered
The scarlet wattle.

Repudiate that blood.
What have we to do with a fear that stalked
In a savage unlit wood?

Time lost! He returned
To limitless space. Storm slept in the leaves,
A dripping sun burned,

And the blood dried
Coursing about his bones. In another fur
That bright beast died.

Yet gaunt—bone, guts, sinews—
Something like man pursued
And still pursues

What? Wheel of the sun
In heaven? The west wind? Or only a will
To his own destruction?

1936

IV. O Pioneers!

The white sagebrush desert. Noon.
All day heat. But the nights cool. And
Again yellowing dawn. Aspens on
Mountains and yellow sagebrush on sand.

Blind light bewilders. Blown or trampled out,
You cannot follow in the apparent wind
Your father's footsteps. It is to this end
They must have led you. Turn and turn about,

The way is lost to fortune. Forward, back,
Delirium will never find a stream
Running gold sands. Rather the earth will crack
Dry on skeletons, skulls in some daft scheme,

Sockets of eyes that perished crazily,
Ignorant of sun, the sagebrush, mad
Even to the dew. A continent they had
To ravage, and raving romped from sea to sea.

1936

THE SAINTS

I

Starveling they trooped
As skeletons
Or as men escaped
Into mere bones,

In hope and rage,
As who would say
All that has age
We must wither away!

And with short steps
On sandspawn and windrack
Staggered. Their lips
Shrivelled black.
The louse was famished
In their hair,
And on ribs unfleshed
The heart-beat bare.

A holy, void
Heat-silvered sky
Had not destroyed
One unlidded eye.
Dark eyes were burnt
To great holes that saw
Visions that were not
Africa.

II

Caesar's crown
Leaf by leaf shed,
Laurels disown
The immortal head.
They cried: Let us stretch
To the scorpion
This dying itch
Of generation!

Motionless
To the flies of noon

Stretched nakedness.
Pocked like the moon
With extinct rock
Desolately expands
To every look
Bright waste of sands.

No cloud emerges
To dissipate despair.
Remorse urges
The sun's glare,
Sharpens the edge
Of a father's fault,
On the bare ledge
Of black basalt.

Subduing time
In naked trance,
Construe as crime
Continuance,
All that changes
Confound with scorn.
So each man avenges
A child born.

III

The gods alone
Know not age, or the grave.
Sea confronts stone.
Caesar cannot save
Cities, sculptures,
Or a boy's blood.
Only endures
The unchanging god.

IV

Blue kiln of day
And brutal fire
Can but allay
Immortal desire.
The desert rock
Stretching to south
Can only mock
The saint's drouth.

O concreate
And never abandoned
Longing! Dilate
Our loves beyond
All loves that age
Or lust consumes,
O thirst and rage
For the lost kingdoms!

Whoever says
Divine has said
Dying. Always
Is a word for the dead.
Shall not bone
Blanched by vision
Desire its own
Lowly dominion?

So that dying thinned
In an alien land,
Wrapped by the wind
In mummying sand,
Can but mitigate
Excess of breath,
While we await
The god in death.

V

I am haunted by
Silence in the sun,
An African eye
Singed by its vision,
On naked sand
Of the dry desert,
Death-longing sustained
By a dying heart.

Saints can commit
Burning excess
In the thorn thicket
Of the sun's wilderness,
At divine cost
Thinned to a breath
That the wind can exhaust
In the sun's wrath.

1935

THE SWORD DANCE

Thunder! In golden clamor they tread the clouds
    Dancing, a burnish of youths—their changing lustres
Move in a tumult of light, their pointed swords
    Touch to the sound of rain, outdistanced by thunder.

Swift armor is chiselled in gilt mythologies:
    Gorgeous the cuirasses—less bright than the gleaming
Ankles, the golden thighs than the leaping knees.
    Their eyes are alight, their mouths are a shout, they
                        are demons.

All have one age, not one of them but is young.
   Vying in violence, they conflict without anger,
Triumphant in thunder. They are dead, being deathless,
                             but strong
As we dying are not, long deaf to their clangor.

They have not dropped their swords; their comeliness
   Is unchanging, their fruitfulness still to garner.
They turn like one form in a circling abyss of glass
    Reflecting the glittering feet, the less bright armor.

1932

ALL'S BRAVE THAT YOUTH MOUNTS

I like young men
Prompt to destroy,
Resentful youth
And prodigal boy,
Pricking such life
In recalcitrant loins
They are careless of all
Embittered coins,
Alexander's race
Ambitious of sun,
Mounted and spurred
For destruction.

Let them swim to master
In harsh salt
Not a cold element
But a body's fault,
Endangered ride
To acquit delight
In the pressed thigh
And perfect bit,
Excellent boys!

86

Acquiring skill
In a waste of sun
And expense of will.
Let them come when strong
To a set face
Deliberate toward death,
Unenvious of grace.

But a man must cry
What no youth can admit:
No star survives
Out of its orbit!
Must cry the stars
That revolving wheel
Around their suns
In consent of will.

1936

A FRIEZE

Arrested like marble horses
In timeless prancing: in the heave of haunches
A pause in the prancing:
Arrested like marble horses, spurred
By impetuous riders, by furious young heels
In a tumultuous curve of haunches.
Confounding seasons,
To the despair of Apollo,
The light on the restless arrested horses, the stayed
Feet, and the beautiful impetuous riders.
Love longs for life, love looks toward ecstasy.
But though the passionate motion ceases
Desire is incensed and urges
The sport for which immortality leases
This extravagant, time's prodigal body

87

With thoughts that exult though the body tire
Appeased but afflicted
With a pain of dissolute longing
Saved from diluvium of timelessness. Whence comes
This rage? Dimensionless and undiminishable
Lust of the timeless prancing, pause in the proud
      prancing,
Spurred by the furious heels of immortal horsemen?

1936

HECUBA'S RAGE

Arrogant and straight, her thought
Concentrate on her body's pride
She entered Troy. There Paris caught
Her, not undying, to his side:
By the lusty act so ecstasied
How could they care what Spartans did?

Ten years of war! They never heard
The street that shrieked the soldier's death.
Cassandra cried. They never stirred
Unless to catch intenser breath.
Far from their rage, Hecuba wept.
They after purer being slept.

On night they cast composite shade,
Half-blinding noon they coupled shone,
Each in the other's presence mad
Until they pressed oblivion.
So gold a summer there was fleshed
Scythings could not be accomplished.

Hecuba waked; distracted, old,
And barren as the dry sea-bed;

For hunger in mean streets had sold
Its child and still cried out for bread:
Piled tumult toward the palace where
Her age must answer to despair.

The crumbling of oppression's roof
Amazed the trophies. Death found speech
In boys' bodies. Put to man's proof
They stretched black lips upon the beach,
Or salt-white in seas' lapse and rise
Assailed her with unburied cries.

And Hecuba wept, queen, barren as
The lone sea-beach. Awake and far
From waste of love Hecuba was!
Only those careless lovers are:
Because of them those wars remain
And Troy, uncrowned of an old queen.

1935

FAREWELL TO MANY CITIES

Nine sea-cities
Of Ilion's lineage
Displaced the seas
And won great wage

In war. Time counterfeits
Change. Their Aprils
Washed violets
Among white hills.

Their summers tanned
Young boys; taught horses
To shadow sand
In hard-run courses.

Their rains were told
In cisterns to ease
The thousand-year-old
Olive trees.

Though oxen lowed
Through distress of drought,
Magnificence flowed
And could not run out.

Stone towers had twice
Concealed their crumblings
Before earth-born mice
Gnawed Teucer's bowstrings.

Dug-over orchards
At times would gape
On painted potsherds
Of outlandish shape.

Can the state be less
Whose thought exults
In the faultlessness
Of its catapults?

Eight sea-cities
Before Ilion shone,
Married to seas.
The ninth is gone.

1935

POOR TOM'S SONG

Alas, to make music I must withdraw
Into a fool's experience.
Only when hair's pranked mad with straw

Do my words make sense.
So night looks for me with shivering crows
Collected on the starving snows.

1936

DIVINE NATIVITY

I

Wisdom that was
Before morning's span
Wheeled into space,
Love in its van,
Through what mishap
Did that Word descend
To a young girl's lap?
And to what end?

II

A god is conceived
In a revel of thighs,
A girl deceived
By descending skies,
On the countenance
Of her visitor
A fallen glance
As of a star.

But a god is born
Of a body's gash
To an old man's scorn,
In pain. What flash
Was there? What fall

Of sudden light
On the animal stall
Of a stabled night?

III

That beauty beheld
At arm's stretch—
That beauty walled—
Beyond our speech
Recreant joy:
A god in play
Or an armored boy,
His bronze cast away.

As the sun shakes
In a strong stare,
Vision partakes
Of that burning air.
O fabled truth!
Did the god's bride
Know an armored youth,
His bronze cast aside?

IV

From beasts the gods came first:
Descending shone in bronze like men,
But found their loves were all accurst
And shook to beasts again.

Adoring Leda leaned upon
A bright encumbrance of wild swan.
Europa rode rejoiced through all
The wild romp of briny bull.

92

Eagle, swan or dove,
White bull or cloud,
Incarnate love
Alone is proud.
The arrogant know
In the bestial part
Overflow
Of the elated heart.

1935

From *SELECTED POEMS*
1941

THAT SUMMER'S END

The yellow wallpaper and the polished floor,
Tall doors that closed upon the afternoon,
Had so subdued the light that once a wasp
Hungry for honey came into that room.

Candles extinct, the crystal sconces made
Slight dissonances with every air that waved
Discreet as light. Old faded curtains could
Remember color in unravelled threads.

It seemed that sullen light could never fade.
Summer was endless as the cicada's drone
That rose to silence and began again
Increasing stridence in a drought of leaves.

Yet all unseen the maples gathered shade
As madness gathers head. None looked. Gusts shook—
And then a sudden looking saw the trees
One shivering silver bending to the storm.

How could we dream the source of light could fail?
Yet, children, we had entertained for years
A madman in that house and never known
How close his motions to delirium

Until that day, after a long drive,
When he came home alone through summer storm
Without a thought that he had left alive,
In a ditch, my mother murdered on the road.

1939

THREE DAYS

Earth opened, by dead thunder riven.
Christ descended, harried Hell.
Unhurried his approach to Heaven,
A place He did not know so well.

1940

LES BALCONS QUI RÊVENT

A sombre green of tropic shade
Early the sleeping shutters made;
The lovers sleep, their dreams increased
By shudders from the night before.

His breath upon his parted lips,
Sleeping he flows into her sleep.
Her belly slumbers, but the tips
Of both dusk breasts are bright awake.

Now winds insist the balcony
Admit its morning to the room,
Restore disorder to the sheets
And chairs by dresses overthrown.

Rustling a green of paradise
The light reflects her opened eyes;
And laughter sees the antique snake
Resume the aspect of a god.

1937

INVITATION AT DAWN

The night has got as far
As the last star.
Venus it is
Who holds the skies
In bold derision
Of the sun.

Surmise what haste
Makes in the East—
O love, my love, let Love invade
Us! Be obeyed
The golden importunity
Of the sky!

For the sun wars
With reserve of years,
Scrupulous to destroy
A small unruly joy,
All time contending
And our love unending.

1941

INTERIOR

Suns from reflected pear-trees scarcely poured
Through windows crossed by wires and overscreened
With shadows from a wall of creeping vines;

Rather, the lustrous walnut sideboard seemed
Reflection from the darker polished floors,
Though raised in carved pear-clusters, leaves and fruit;

Until with creaking doors the sideboard swung
On autumn lasting in unfrosted pears
And longer summer stored on musty shelves:

99

Globed gooseberries translucent in a cool
Suspense of seeded green; black opaque grape;
And ruby radiance from small currants fused;

That savage, mountain-gathered, scuppernong;
Crabapple tarter than the quince; wild tang
Of dewberries clambering a fallen fence.

Their odors sullen under paper caps,
The child discovered that the room distilled
A secret mould and mawkish smell of wax;

And through it all—glass-cruets, table set
Always for another meal, the peacock bunch—
The closely guarded death of family walls.

1937

CONQUEST OF THE WIND

That John beyond the Rock Bridge, in his own blood,
Retraced the savage. Anne, when the forest dawn
Surprised her doorway, smiled, as her brother
Followed the moccasins of a mocking sun.

To Primrose of the block house, all the spring
Of flowers brought only bloodroot. That other John
Under the shadow of the Massanutten
Drank from the coldest streams a bloodied shade.

The nameless many whom I do not name,
Packed upon horseback, came where mountain trail
Pressed thickets of laurel and a wilderness of May
Broke like a promise in unbroken bloom.

Our past is in the ground and not the blood:
Forbidden, my fathers to that valley came
Seeking the freedom of unfailing springs
And trees beyond the trees the savage burned.

Tall sycamores peered out, sun-spotted fawns.
The willows half-existed in a gleam.
They found their forests and undid their packs,
They set their hearts down by a shelving stream.

Because of them I was set down by streams.
Incarnate in that ancient choice, I stood
By streams where boyhood, like a heron, shyly
Stares at green silence through long afternoons.

Stout bodies, hooped by stronger skeletons,
Strong ribs and sturdy to outlast the heart,
They bred in fury to increase their graves.
No greater hope hollowed their solitude.

Not all: there were still those who could not stick
By any hearthstone, but must stir their fires
Where none but the reflected panther's eyes
Could see the blaze upon their lonely hands.

None saw, when morning rose, for forests round
Their wisps of smoke above the wild treetops.
They found their fortune in a buckskin day
By merely following a western cloud.

My long since born and now abandoned bones
Are scattered, white dust, about this continent,
America a passage of the sun,
A crossing and a conquest of the wind.

And I in sun am shadowed by blue hills,
Because of boyhood brambled by old stains,
Blackberry memories of meadow heat.
From confines of the ground such fathers creep,

Escape, and gilding stones as gliding silt
Run courses confluent to the Shenandoah,
Or pile as driftwood by the flooded shores
And willow islands of the rising stream.

The nameless many whom I do not name
Have scattered names above the thousand miles,
Once the mad pleasure of a western air
And now dispersed upon the storms they made.

The divagations of the wandering will
Are long the devastations of the wind.
Let the curlew cry or the trumpeter swan,
If any cry, let those doomed throats proclaim

The triumph of that space-destroying rage!
Let the wild swan on glittering wings return,
Outstretched as on a space of cloud, and cry
The anguish of its race and vanished range!

Our past is in the ground and not the blood.
Descended from the generations of those graves,
Let me a little while pluck a green pride
Before the lightning burns the stricken leaves.

1937

THE "YANKEE TRADER"

An old sofa has been abandoned
At the *Yankee Trader*, an old sofa
Has been left out in the snow.

Slightly lopsided, it still proposes
With its faded roses positions for courtships
Proper and posied against the snow.

With its sodden roses under the snow
And its stiff scrolls, the sofa recovers
The stiffer backs and the sobbing postures:

A coffin treading on legs through doors,
A family fading into the snow.
The doors are closed on the *Yankee Trader.*

An old sofa, coldly abandoned,
Might still support, more patient than lovers,
The fall of snow on its final roses,

Outstaying men, may still withstand
Eternal fault in the falling elements,
A stiff wind and the approaching snow.

1940

PHAETON

This is the hour the youngest dread
Through the dark dared and longed-for hour
When the untried youth starts from his bed,
For the thronged Pleiads lower
And the bright horses display their power.

He knows what fierceness orbs the sun,
Annihilating grace of fire,
And dreads the god's descent upon
The uncurbed plungings of desire,
The son that imitates the sire.

1941

EROS

Winged god, who through the dark hours grieved,
Now that the light is in the east,
Preen your proud plumes, your joy achieved
Through torture of composite beast.

1941

WHY THEY WAGED WAR

> *De cela, M. de Coquet ne retient*
> *qu'une chose: c'est que la guerre de*
> *Troie a lieu, quoiqu'on tente pour*
> *l'empêcher.*

It's clear, Trojan cried out to Greek,
You've chosen Troy as your prey.
Not at all, called back Agamemnon,
Your Paris took Helen away.

It is not wise, said Ulysses,
To have gods so covered with gold.
And worse, in his palace sighed Priam,
To be gilded and yet grow old.

1939

WHOM THE GODS LOVE

That illustrious thing
Body in all its pride
Cut down: undiminishing
Scaean Achilles died.

Into extolled
Old age, tittering on,
Tithonus terribly recalled
The boy that lay with the dawn.

1940

COLLAPSE OF TIME

Mills closed, doors shut, windows empty
Except for stones; mills closed, doors shut, dispelling
    Wanderers, some or none to hear
    Gnaw of machines again.

Ducks flew in vain to the drain marshes. Crows
Crossed, drought cropped, a starved and lowing pasture.
    Here greed was changed to devastation,
    At last to a fixed conceit of fear.

Climate changed: cut woods, loosed floods
Ravaged the valleys; distant storms
    Accumulated dust in tall cities,
    The ancient cupola'd capitol topped

By a silent elevation of steel girders,
Minium-painted giddiness, from which all men
    Were gone; all work stopped; the noonday sun
    Was dusked to red by dust-clouds.

Streets rose, strikers rioted. Was one who sat
Transcolored by his own failure, though starving
    White and whole with rage, under
    The air-pawing horses of descending

Law, a long age of disinherited terror, before
The clubbed skull rolled in torment. Brute
    Hoofbeats clattered about the empty square.
    Corpses sprouted from dead clothes on pavement stones.

The contemplation of all action waits
On opinion. We are governed in our own despite

But by our own disorder. Dissemblers
Deceive us with our own words.

Time does not lack for instruments of torture.
Interpreters attain hysteria. Men are voices.
    The lately spat-on, become our tyrants,
    Punish both the faults of the blood

And blood running. Our new Caesar is crowned
By old newspapers. Look closely! You will see
    His oppressive sceptre has been rolled
    From a revolutionary manifesto.

1936

TRINITY OF CRIME

Who is this that is hammered upon the hands
And hammered hard into the thin foot-bone?
Who is this, heaved upward to the heavens,
        Stares so alone?

Two thieves that were black blood upon the cheek-bone
Are now thrust up all black against the sky,
And twisted thighs, foul mouths, and broken noses
        Begin to die.

Darkness whirls upon a might of thunder
And the wind's green within a murk of sun.
Soldiers lift their spears—piercing, consume
        Crucifixion.

Who is this whose face is fallen sickly,
Whose hair falls when his last cry is spent
In an agony of failure? Stretched arms are nailed.
        His knees are bent.

This is the man who damned to dream alone
Dreamed of God's loneliness. His destiny
Upon a place of skulls is ended. He is dead
           And one of three.

JOHN DONNE'S STATUE

> *Upon this urn he thus stood, with
> his eyes shut, and with so much of
> the sheet turned aside as might shew
> his lean, pale and deathlike face, which
> was purposely turned toward the East.*

He threw the shroud about his head
And bade the sculptor come.
Present me to proud Death, he said,
As one long known and overcome.
Disclose beneath these cerements
His love congealing every sense.
I shall stand giddy on the tomb.

Proud Donne was one did not believe
In heirs presumptive to a bone
Or boys' pursuit of love, their leave
To sensual oblivion.
Come dying then! Too fine a joy
And too intrinsic for a boy:
Sustain that ecstasy in stone!

How strangely now that figure stirs,
And strange the smile appears,
Distracting all the sepulchres
Drowsed with their dust three hundred years.
In death, that disillusion
Becomes as sensual as the sun
Whose laurel a green summer wears.

1938

THE STATUE OF A SHADOW *

This was that mystery of clearest light:
No cloud,
No shadow of a cloud
Passed on the stretch where then I stood.
A sandy noon consumed my sight.

I saw my body cast
In shadow and was afraid.
I saw time vast
As my own shadow and was afraid.
In light and a vision of light
I saw my shadow cast
Upon that coast.
The shade of all those centuries
Where death is longing and fate a crime
Lay long
But no longer
Than the statue of a shadow
Noon laid at my feet.
This was that mystery:
Time had no other feature.

1939

COLLOQUY WITH A KING-CRAB

Dwarf pines; the wild plum on the wind-grassed shore
Shaken by autumn to its naked fruit;
Visions of bright winds across the bay:
These are, perhaps, sufficient images
To say what I have sought. These I have found.
Let these suffice with seas—though honesty is this,
To know what's sought from what the sands have found.

---

* Another, presumably earlier version of this poem appears as section V of
"The Statues," page 160.

It needs no Proteus to announce the sea
Above the proclamations of loud surf—
Only the horseshoe crab, black carapace,
Project of life, though hideous, persisting
From the primordial grasp of claws on shore.
This crab is no abstraction, yet presents
No difficulty to the abstract mind,
His head all belly and his sword a tail,
But to the imagination is suspect.
Reject him? Why? Though voiceless, yet he says
That any monster may remain forever
If he but keep eyes, mind and claws intent
On the main chance, be not afraid to skulk.
This proletarian of the sea is not,
But scuttles, noble as the crocodile,
As ancient in his lineage. His name
Is not unknown in heaven. But his shell
Affords no edifice where I can creep
Though I consent like him to go on claws.

1938

UNCOLLECTED POEMS

1937-1945

UNCOLLECTED POEMS

FOURTEEN

This is the boy whose sleep was filled with birds,
  Who sightless followed where the day had gone
Beyond the dogwood of a mountain stream:
His sleep was as his days a singing green,

A shade disturbed by Guatemalan gleams:
Redstarts alert upon the thicket, shy
Yellowthroats, black maskers of the undergrowth.
All praised that punctual miracle of May.

When love like a wind stirs from the South,
And all the anguish of the world is winged,
Mayapples hide their root and judas bud
Betrays the blood within the wilderness.

But most he sought those birds he had not seen:
Sleep's scarlet ibises, in Floridas
Unreached; flamingoes with a stately tread
Among imagined sea-sands, storms of palm.

1937

A CHARM

Chicamy—chicamy—crany—crow

If the sun recover
Each girl shall have a lover,

Boys ease their blood
In the gay laurel wood.

Chicamy—chicamy—crany—crow

Shall be seen, both day and night,
Symptoms of a flushed delight.
All shall have simplicity
Faith and fame of chastity.

I went to the well to wash my toe

What time is it, old witch?

1937

THE HOURS *

*In the real dark night of the soul it is always three o'clock
in the morning.*—F. Scott Fitzgerald

I

All day, knowing you dead,
I have sat in this long-windowed room,
Looking upon the sea and, dismayed
By mortal sadness, though without thought to resume
Those hours which you and I have known—
Hours when youth like an insurgent sun
Showered ambition on an aimless air,
Hours foreboding disillusion,
Hours which now there is none to share.
Since you are dead, I leave them all alone.

II

A day like any day. Though any day now
We expect death. The sky is overcast,
And shuddering cold as snow the shoreward blast.

* This poem was printed in *The New Republic*, March 3, 1941, among other
tributes to the memory of F. Scott Fitzgerald.

And in the marsh, like a sea astray, now
Waters brim. This is the moment when the sea
Being most full of motion seems motionless.
Land and sea are merged. The marsh is gone.
And my distress
Is at the flood. All but the dunes are drowned.
And brimming with memory I have found
All hours we ever knew, but have not found
The key. I cannot find the lost key
To the silver closet you as a wild child hid.

III

I think of all you did
And all you might have done, before undone
By death, but for the undoing of despair.
No promise such as yours when like the spring
You came, colors of jonquils in your hair,
Inspired as the wind, when the woods are bare
And every silence is about to sing.

None had such promise then, and none
Your scapegrace wit or your disarming grace;
For you were bold as was Danaë's son,
Conceived like Perseus in a dream of gold.
And there was none when you were young, not one,
So prompt in the reflecting shield to trace
The glittering aspect of a Gorgon age.

Despair no love, no fortune could assuage . . .
Was it a fault in your disastrous blood
That beat from no fortunate god,
The failure of all passion in mid-course?
You shrank from nothing as from solitude,
Lacking the still assurance, and pursued
Beyond the sad excitement by remorse.

Was it that having shaped your stare upon
The severed head of time, upheld and blind,
Upheld by the stained hair,
And seen the blood upon that sightless stare,
You looked and were made one
With the strained horror of those sightless eyes?
You looked, and were not turned to stone.

IV

You have outlasted the nocturnal terror,
The head hanging in the hanging mirror,
The hour haunted by a harrowing face.
Now you are drunk at last. And that disgrace
You sought in oblivious dives you have
At last, in the dissolution of the grave.

V

I have lived with you the hour of your humiliation.
I have seen you turn upon the others in the night
And of sad self-loathing
Concealing nothing
Heard you cry: *I am lost. But you are lower!*
And you had that right.
The damned do not so own their damnation.

I have lived with you some hours of the night,
The late hour
When the lights lower,
The later hour
When the lights go out,

When the dissipation of the night is past,
Hour of the outcast and the outworn whore,
That is past three and not yet four—

116

When the old blackmailer waits beyond the door
And from the gutter with unpitying hands
Demands the same sad guiltiness as before,
The hour of utter destitution
When the soul knows the horror of its loss
And knows the world too poor
For restitution,
                    Past three o'clock
And not yet four—
                    When not pity, pride,
Or being brave,
Fortune, friendship, forgetfulness of drudgery
Or of drug avails, for all has been tried,
And nothing avails to save
The soul from recognition of its night.

The hour of death is always four o'clock.
It is always four o'clock in the grave.

VI

Having heard the bare word that you had died,
All day I have lingered in this lofty room,
Locked in the light of sea and cloud,
And thought, at cost of sea-hours, to illume
The hours that you and I have known,
Hours death does not condemn, nor love condone.

And I have seen the sea-light set the tide
In salt succession toward the sullen shore
And while the waves lost on the losing sand
Seen shores receding and the sands succumb.

The waste retreats; glimmering shores retrieve
Unproportioned plunges; the dunes restore
Drowned confines to the disputed kingdom—
Desolate mastery, since the dark has come.

The dark has come. I cannot pluck you bays,
Though here the bay grows wild. For fugitive
As surpassed fame the leaves this sea-wind frays.
Why should I promise what I cannot give?

I cannot animate with breath
Syllables in the open mouth of death.
Dark, dark. The shore here has a habit of light.
O dark! I leave you to oblivious night!

1941

RESURRECTION

I saw the body on the cross
Restored to motion, surge with blood.
Whatever is, I saw this was
The resurrection of a god.

The tree that had been dead was quick
Resurgent branches every one
Broke into green, and air was thick
With leaves all crowding toward the sun.

Rustling like flames, the leaves went up
And when the sun came down to gild
Tree from the ground to glittering top
Wounds in the hands and feet were healed.

The limbs turned bright with sun among
Green against gold and on gold fire
Body of death, recovered, young
With all the portents of desire

Ambiguous brightness of a boy
Not yet a man, yet all a god
For none but god could find his joy
In death perpetually renewed.

118

The resurrection and the death
Reversed their passage on the tree
The soul surrendering its breath
Returned into its secrecy

So lucid was that suffering
In leaves! Of one wound the god died
And all the undyings of the spring
Decked from the wound within his side.

1941

OCCUPATION OF A CITY

> *Méfiez-vous, amis, du silence qui*
> *précède de tels événements.*

Silence of the conquered city,
The silences:

Silence of the *tricouleur*
In an air crowned by the deposed doves.
The silent ministries: burned archives
And the charred litter of belated decisions.

Silence of the *triporteur*
Trundling bread to a depleted courtyard:
Doors opening on dark passageways
From which it is no longer possible to depart.

Solemnity of the balconies:
Secret listeners; and shutters closed upon those
Who sulk in terror at the throb of troops,
The paced pulsations of invading blood.

Silence of the besiegers:
For the city is still besieged
By the army of the betrayed, the vile, the brave
In their various disguises as dead men.

The commander silent in his car,
His memory a map of tomorrow.
Abashment of the trophies: ambitious arms
Massed in marble to adorn the sky:
Helpless shields, empty helmets, lowered standards,
The crest armor of a depraved glory.

Restraint of the statues: the troops proceeded,
The rumble of troops proceeded amid the mute
Reproach of munificent columns, which alone
Mounted guard on the immense and deserted square.

Rode on carriages of cannon
In imperturbable postures. The stare of statues—
Sequence of light on stone—the civic crowns
Disowned by the lost cities. Astride horses.

Suspicion the shadow on their eyelids
Under the shade of helmets. With no sound
But their own, proceeded to the occupation
Of a city already occupied by silence.

1941

A SUBJECT OF SEA CHANGE

The Phi Beta Kappa Poem

Columbia University, June 1, 1942

I

I have built my house amid sea-bitten green,
Among the pitch pines of a dispersed wood;

The winters of five years it has withstood
Incessant winds and in the salt air been
Bleached in its shingles to a silvery grey,
Which even now, when spring is overhead,
Answers from thickets of unwakened bay.

Along this coast, thickets of wild bay abound
With leaves as bitter as worn fame would be,
Did not the inveterate winters intervene
To strip and scatter all the blackened green;
Yet here no mortal head was ever crowned;
Along the sea, courage alone is praised;
Only the sea adorns the dissolute drowned.

The bay resumes abstract mortality,
Bleached branches breaking from a sandy ground,
As penetrable as the dead
Who wildly clamored round
The sacrificial pit for the spilt blood
And were not eased before Tiresias came
To his dread repast from the slain ram.

No need to pour our black blood on the sand.
The multitude of the dead is now too easily raised.
Yet should they come
They would, though the heart lift and beat, be dumb.
Even if he should come at last
Upon his golden staff, stumbling and blind,
Tiresias, who, among the shifting dead,
Has high repute for holding a steadfast mind,
Who'd listen, should he come, though all he said
Were borne in words rare and profound,
Unbodied voices being unused to sound?
Who listens now to the hoarse speech of the dead,
Or heeds predictions from a derelict past?

I have built my house upon these ancient sands
Swept shoreward from the sea and beyond the shore,
Spurned sea-loss adding to the spume-lost store
Ten thousand years or more,
Until what was the sea's remains the land's.
I chose this outlook on the changeable sea,
After much voyaging, to find
Not calm, for calm's a constant of the mind,
But in this sea-changed air a constancy—
Like a man's look contracted where he loves—
To hold in instant contemplation
The shifting flow of human history
That seaward sets even as it shoreward moves.

I choose this strange inconstant coast,
Where all is won and lost,
Lost and again won,
As though each day were present at creation.
What if the long breakwaters amplify the land,
The sea retire before a widening strand,
When the great waters break? Then all once more is change
And again change. The oldest contours
Of these refluent shores
Are subject always to the sea's revenge.

Here we are so far flung out
Into the spacious seas, we cannot choose but know
How all things come about and about.
Sharper than any gale's tang on the cheek we feel
Sensuously the seasonable wheel:
Know the delayed spring's silvery advance
And autumn's soon retiring golden rout
Are largess in a long extravagance.

Sea-ravished senses easily conceive
What else had been an unquickened thought
Which all acknowledge and none quite believe,
That every ordered change of form
Brings winds' disorder and destroying storm.

Alert to all this natural ebb and flow,
I thought I should be taught to bear
In the salt shudder of this sea-borne air
The fall and flood that's fatal to our history.
The sea, like remorse, is everywhere
And its great wrecks have long surviving spars.
Between two worlds betrayed, between two wars,
I've had no sadder thing to bear than change,
No darker thing than night,
No more dread sight
Than warriors to whom honor is strange.

I must learn again the great part of Man—
Though the lines are scant that any man may speak—
Proclaiming with such passion as I can
The part first played, and nobly, by a Greek.
Time is man's tragic responsibility
And on his back he bears
Both the prolific and destroying years.
And so, I swear, he must surround each act
With scruples that will hold intact
Not merely his own, but human, dignity.
Let him not fall into our common fault
Which is to ignore stains of corroding salt—
Let me not wash my actor's mask of tears!

I long to get on with the play—
But then in the background I hear the great bombs drop
And suddenly tremble lest the long play stop

And only throned statues of the great survey
A reign of rubble in a littered day.

III

Noon's brilliance strains through cobalt streaks
To spread in azure and pale light beyond.
If blue were all, this were the sea where Greeks
Squatted like Plato's frogs about a pond.
The sea, the sea, burns with antiquity.

There was a sea cast gods from its surf like spray,
Salt on their lips, the animation
On their faces like the light
Of an invisible joy, the brightness of their breath
Not from the stiff and breathing surge, and they
Knotted their hands in the wild manes of horses
And the horses emerged from the waves, stranger
And stronger than the leaping waves, and came
Trampling like light upon the shore and there,
Stilling their trembling in the luminous air,
Were mused to marvels of untroubled stone.

On what indeed does all our state depend
But on the architecture of the waves,
That staring whiteness where no whiteness stays,
Sequence of waves that signify no end
Unless it be, under the harassing wind,
To hasten toward the shore and overwhelm
The old division of the gods' dominion?
The sea is subject to another realm.

The need for order first created gods
Immortal, then gave them generation,
Since every god is unthroned by his son,
And a deposed god is a cruel fantasy.

124

So every order that the mind's conceived
Conceives its own corruption.
The oldest god was soon forgotten
When his potent members sank into the sea.
I look upon another sea
And now the world's confounded into odds
And state is mutilated or achieved.
Remember how Love came on the immediate swell
Reflecting in a shiver of resplendent spray
The dawn enclosed within her secret shell.
No other god has held so visible a sway.

IV

Death greets us all without civility
And every color of the sea is cold,
Even as now, when sensual greens advance
Under the contrary waves' propensity
Toward desirable blues. The sea is old,
Severe and cold, secret as antiquity
Under the scud of time. And the sea rants,
Storm-crossed, thunder-tossed,
Yet has a poetry so profound
That none but the unwaxed ear to the mast bound
Should hear it, or it may be the lost
Long-listening bodies of the drowned.

1942

THE SUBMARINE BED

Children conceived when two nightgowns
In a bold clasp confused the bed . . .
As when an encumbered body drowns
And drowning lifts a dreadful head,

Each head was drawn to a strict tilt
To have no part in what was done,
While the lost gowns assumed the guilt
That should have been the body's own.

Bodies in deeper being plunged,
Abandoned sightless to the flood,
Swept down. Those two gowns lunged
Like hungry dogfish after food

That fled. Love? Was it love expulsed
To where those shrouds of love were wound
On corpses which with limbs convulsed
Sank into seas yet more profound?

Concupiscent, those gowns attain
The end they coveted. Their heads stare
Sightless at mortality, then
Strain at the incorporeal air.

After such turmoil and such lust,
After such wreckage in the bed,
It is not easy to adjust
The body to a severed head.

1944

GHOULS' WHARF

A shanty of the shingled sort
Had let him out to freeze his tears.
A lone gull brought a shrill report
Of a lost sea beyond the piers
To an old man on Ghouls' Wharf.

His frozen sight in fog was lost,
And all beyond the piles was gone.
"Out of a cloud the waves are tossed,
For now the sea and cloud are one,"
Said the old man on Ghouls' Wharf.

Driving toward dissolution,
Waves were denied upon the shore.
"Haled to light by the ghost of a sun,
What are the damned so harried for,
That they should hasten toward Ghouls' Wharf?

"I've seen them come, drawn by a need
To end their own damnation,
Already damned when their sires' seed
Sprang to their generation,"
Sang the old man on Ghouls' Wharf.

"Reversing still the course of waves,
They crowd like ghosts. In unison,
They cry like ghosts whom nothing saves
In the white absence of the sun
That chills the gulls upon Ghouls' Wharf.

"I never know if they're the drowned
Sloughed by the sea or if they have
Stark memories of being bound
To secrets in the earth's conclave,"
Said the old man on Ghouls' Wharf.

"They wait the tide and never know
How for them all time's run out.
And what is time to me? The snow
Wafts a white blindness all about.
I stare at nothing from Ghouls' Wharf.

"I might have called up sea-blue crowds
Or gods that scale from green to bronze.
But what should I do, old man, with gods
Whose glory to their guilt responds?"
Cried the old man on Ghouls' Wharf.

1944

THE PARALLEL

The tide comes in along the track
That the sun takes; the sands give way
Before the sea's dividing wrack,
And both deploy before dividing day.

The sea filled with that might but holds
More of the sea and falls replete
With fortune. The sand flees and moulds
Sandy monuments to its own defeat.

Antony, when all ships lit out,
Had his heart's desire. He had loved the East
And now the East had deserted him; a rout
Of ships surrounded him. He was increased

And stood alone in a great glare
Where all his honor hung on choice—
Moment melodious and rare
As when the tortoise lifts his voice—

Being surcharged with being, a brute
Made bright by armor, brimming gold
Into the air, and absolute
Upon the deserted heart, but old

In exaltation of the will;
Where nothing fails that falls by chance
His fate was vile, but visible,
And his soul stronger for the glance.

There fled an hundred Antonies,
But the heroic stood alone,
Where nothing past or future is
And the whole sea scatters on a stone.

1944

THE SPARE QUILT

An art as meagre as a quilt
Of faded colors, oddly matched
From flowers which fading could not wilt
Though to a white like winter's patched.

They pieced, they interlined and stitched,
Since nature would not keep them warm;
And close at night their shoulders twitched
The quilt about them when the storm

Outraged the windows and outside
Shrieked in the uncharitable air.
They knew then that the night was wide
And wished their art had been less spare.

But as the long night settled down,
Shivering from chill to chill,
They felt the darkness like a frown
And felt their work had not been ill.

Hugging the quilt they saw how young
Indulgent hunters shining went
Toward danger, proud, and most when hung
With death, their souls sufficient

To that solitude. It solaced them
That those unshivering sons were stout,
Since they, contented with a dream,
Could only stitch the cold night out.

1944

THE DREAM

And once again I was within that house
Where light collided with the gloom
And chilled on faces, as though the dawn
Were backward and the stars had gone;
For the long hall was populous
With pale expatriates from the tomb.

The house, deserted, had become a lair,
And all along that hall the dead slid
And tried the doors, one after one,
With hands no longer blest by bone.
They scanned me with a single stare
Because of what that one door hid.

I saw my mother, who had love
Still in her eyes, that did not own
Least light, for they had forfeited
Reflection, having reached the dead.
She spoke: and I was conscious of
An unspoken corruption.

Her speech prevented me from following
Angrily after those famished forms
Who only sought what I had sought
And found. I had been brought,
In the dread time of love's responding,
Undreaming into my young love's arms.

I saw what they were seeking in the gust
That drove them on from door to door
In the long deception of the hall.
They looked: from doors, nothing at all
Looked back at them. Yet though no lust
Awaited them, they must try once more.

I saw the shame that I contemned
Since it was sought by sightless eyes.
I knew what crime would be revealed
If the one door to the dead should yield,
But dreamed that door had been condemned
And in the dream had no surprise.

That none could ever force a look
At incest dangling from a beam
And by a cord all blood attached.
For from the dark I knew there watched
Young eyes too quick with love to mock
The dead in that death-haunted dream.

1945 *

* This, the last of Bishop's serious poems, was written, in the late spring of
1943. His last poem, a piece of light verse, "To Richard Powell, To Amuse,"
written in the summer of 1943, remained unpublished at the time of his death
(see page 167).—Editor.

UNPUBLISHED LATER POEMS

1925-1943

UNPUBLISHED LATER POEMS

SAINT FRANCIS

The curé in his windy gown
   Wildly stops and lifts his sleeves
To bless the flight that flutters down,
Late yellow flock of beechen leaves.

Bewildered by their wings he stands
And overcomes the wind with words,
An old daft man with helpless hands,
Saint Francis preaching to the birds.

Cir. 1932

NATIVITY

Conceived in no revel
Of lovers confused
By their own loveliness
To prompt seed and unbless
An innocent cell,
But brought forth, bruised
In his being, born
To the straw-rank smell
Of an animal stall
And an old man's scorn,
The son of light
Gropes earthward again.

135

Light's conception
On careless clay
To the loud delight
Of the seraphim,
Above is a woman
Who smiles at Him,
Beside Him a man
Who looks away.

Cir. 1940

ARS AMATORIS

Never abandon thought
Unless for ecstasies!
Even when you are brought
To where your blest love lies,
With all her bright hair flung
In the abandonment of the young.

Lucifer from his bright place
Fell. Beside the sun
He had lacked no luminous grace
Or compelling passion:
Despoiled of the proud east,
He tumbled and crawled a beast.

Cir. 1925

APRIL IN ORGEVAL

It is not that jonquils point with yellow petals
The nimble winds of morning as they run,
That the cuckoo's loud, chestnuts
Proclaim green leaves; nor that the night,
Deprived of Pleiades, imparts the whippoorwill;
And fruit-trees cannot save their branches
But all that quickening fire is white in clusters;

Thyme has silver scent again; and children
Hurrying to catch golden cowslips
Sink in sun, and humble knees to grasses;
Nor even that now, in woods, dead rotted leaves
Have all a wild odor of violets: for none
Of these; but that now and for the eleventh
April, your smile becomes more beautiful,
I know that it is Spring.

Cir. 1933

BAROQUE

I looked on those who are dead and were proud:
Content with blood, in what contempt of breath
By the encherubed stairs, under painted cloud,
Some paced on rose reflections to the death!

But most I think in pride upon those Anthonies:
The Roman, stalked by thirst, who for his gilt
Helmet shouted and, admired by armies, drank stale piss
With carelessness, as though an empire spilt.

Or on that African, another Anthony,
Exalted by the desert, who sat and would not nod
For fear lest dreams should bring worse visions. He
Could stiffen his neck to every thought but God.

Cir. 1928

"PAOLO UCCELLO'S BATTLE HORSES . . ."

Paolo Uccello's battle horses' hooves
First roused this tumult which assaults our ears,
This calumny of time, this spacious rage
Which every dusty fool now thinks he hears.

The young men and the pennons are upraised,
Superb in embattled space, a charger rears
Haunches surpassing hours of men and spears.

Now Einstein's head is wearier than age;
Night dies; and sun alone the morning proves.
But dawn shall hear those mighty buttocks praised.

Cir. 1928

THE PROMISE

The thief on the third cross was not forever good
For he reviled his dying god. Yet his live eyes
Dying as man, not god, revealed he had withstood
The torture of extinction. That is paradise.

Cir. 1928

"BOYS, BY GIRLS HELD IN THEIR THIGHS"

Boys, by girls held in their thighs,
Shudder, and turn back their eyes.
It is as well they never see
The brute approach of ecstasy.

Cir. 1928

"GEORGE WASHINGTON USED TO DRIVE"

(A Fragment)

George Washington used to drive
through the hills of Virginia
in a costly carosse ordered from London
painted sea-green, the doors and panels
curling into gold just lifted from the sea.

Poor Washington! when he died
his tomb was cut to his measure
of antique marble. You may see him still
in the forecourt of the Capitol
his toga over his knees,
noble, republican, Roman.

I knew his family well,
having been born on land which the General
somehow or other got out of Lord Fairfax
and gave to his brothers. I knew them all—
the granddaughter of Betty Lewis,
the descendants of Charles, of Samuel's six
        consorts—
particularly I knew Sheldon Washington
whose father had been born at Mount Vernon.
They were none of them in the least Roman,
though Sheldon might, had he known Latin,
have quoted Petronius at thirteen:
Iunonem meam iratam habeam
si unquam me meminerim virginem fuisse . . .

Cir. 1928

"BUT NOW I LOOK UPON THE CALENDAR"

But now I look upon the calendar
And wonder how it is
I have come so close to Death.
No need to ask where devil's foot
Or lost years are.
To me, to anyone
Death answers one and only one
Question. To who proposes
When? He, after a pause, says *Now!*

Cir. 1930

DRUNK AND UNPARDONABLE

The delicate young man, whose grandfathers had fought
At Culloden, Yorktown, Gettysburg and Chancellorsville,
Whose father had made money
In Akron, Bridgeport, Boston and Pittsburgh,
Came out of the speakeasy and with difficulty
Adjusted his face to a look of distaste:
Said: They have no grandfathers
And they are already pederasts.

Cir. 1930

POEM OF FOUR LINES WITH THREE TITLES

UNBALANCING THE SCALES
THE STATUE'S NAME IS JUSTICE
UPON ASSASSINATION AS A MEANS OF SOCIAL REFORM

Be not astonished if, when laurel fails,
The statue at whose base dead Caesar slumps
Outbleeds the victim or lets fall the scales
To hold the sword between two bloody stumps.

Cir. 1932

"HARDER IT IS TO SING . . ."

Harder it is to sing than shout
And rotten, rotten is the age.
But what are all these poets about,
Their throats constricted by their rage?

Cir. 1934

TO A CRITIC

You carried on your trade. You've had your say.
From his high horse dragging the poet down,
You left him viler than the rest of us.
Did not the anger of an arched head, blown
Mane and foreheels prepared for flight betray
His absurd and lofty mount was Pegasus?

Cir. 1934

"THIS CRITIC"

This critic, whose mind
Is so sure in its wit, so precise
In its allotment of praise and blame, is not,
When seen, what you would expect. It moves
About the room, peering, like an old woman
Trying to buy something at a price
Much cheaper than it can possibly be bought.

Cir. 1934

"YOU'D THINK THAT HE WOULD CAUSE A SHOCK"

You'd think that he would cause a shock
The scorpion with his double cock,
Both sides erect, but not at all.
The scorpion is a liberal.

One thrusts to right, one sticks to left
As he advances toward the cleft
And then presents in copulation
The New Republic of the Nation.

Cir. 1934

A GREEN AND PLEASANT LAND

It was strange, O strange
That all this rose
Out of our forests:

Foundries exuding
A new sky: constant sunsets,
Suffocations of smoked cloud.

The fishes died;
Landscapes of slag, acids corroded
The green stream.

Engineers invented
Rapid metallic streams,
Sierras of anthracite, sulphur dawns,

Inhabited by sturdy grimaces
Of grime; besotted men
Who moved their muscles to another's mind.

Cir. 1934

"FOUR NOBLE HORSES . . ."

Four noble horses without sound
Come toward us, crests against the sky.
Their molten hooves disdain the ground
To touch on air or porphyry.

From the steep ledge they covet space
Who own no bounds in cloud or air;
Because no aim was set their race,
They have their being everywhere.

Bronze horses invisibly willed
And brutally set forth in fire,
Such force was in their forms fulfilled
They bound unbated as desire,

Brimming with that bright arrogance
Of those who need no death to come.
He dropped his breath, forgot all chance
Who chose their equilibrium.

Desire invisible as wind
Impels them to the course they run
Immured in metal; disciplined
Against the slow dissolving sun.

For time is thought, and bestial these
Are heirs and loot of time. They slip
Through time as dolphins through the seas,
Superior to the sparks they drip,

Their green bronze diversified
Like the sea's green with brilliant blue.
Death is to motion so allied
They make no motion but in hue.

The stunned light starts in resonance
From the struck hoof.

Cir. 1935

THE EMPEROR ALSO WAS A GOD

What should we do when a world dies?

The centurion charged with the crucifixion
Saw to it that everything was done according to orders
Despite the three women weeping apart
And the fanatic mob that would not leave off its taunting.

The god too did his part
Since his part was to die.

The space about the crosses was at all times kept clear.
The storm that broke from a sulphurous cloud
Helped to disperse the crowd.
The soldiers had only to use the butt-ends of their spears.

No one, the centurion felt, had anything to complain of
    at Golgotha.
The culprits' garments did not amount to much
But then they were something for the soldiers to cast
    dice for.

What should we weep for when a world is dying?

The emperor's statue
Enormous as a god's, in an empty forum,
Waited, naked in its armor, forays of the barbarians.

What is there to wait for when a world is dying?
Cir. 1935

NARCISSUS

What could he do above the mirroring stream,
Matching desire with his virginity,
Jostled by green reeds, boy, but sway
Naked and young upon a margin of the
Envious silver? What could he do but plunge
Into those depths where body is a gleam
Continuously passing; where in the intricacies
Of water the yellow-white jonquil is
Rivalled by reflections and in the constancy
Of motion color and form are vanishings?

144

Where the grey leaves of the willow trailing
Are glitters, what could he do but wade
Following the solitary stock of his body
With its circling white drifts of petals? What
Drink but desire? What could he do but burn
Into a contemplation, marvelling
That his own body was become a whirling
Mirror of death? Stark in dissolution
Stare at swifter shadows, flooding, that charged
All changing objects with raging delight?

Cir. 1935

EPITAPH FOR A POET

The verse must never exactly scan
If the poet is a gentleman—
This poet was: he might have either
Made his family a livelihood
Or written odes to praise his blood;
He couldn't do both, so he did neither.
He gasped like a hound in a wayside ditch
Calling the world a son of a bitch;
There he died, refined and thin,
With his small Scottish nose and his large Irish chin.

Cir. 1935

PAST AND PRESENT

I admire Ben Jonson's statement: it is right
To prefer the past to the present since by the one
We are instructed, but by the other
Overwhelmed. I have seen
Great empires overwhelmed. Of Vienna, I remember
The grass growing in the courtyard
Of the Hofburg and under the great staircase
The packing cases ranged, where the poor were not fed;

The starved boy with the speckled face
Listless in front of the library and the drowned girl
In the rowboat slowly oared by the gendarme,
Her hair wet from the Danube,
Her hair soaked and her shame exposed.
And I remember Paris
Walking at midnight under the arcades,
No sound but my own steps
Reverberating under the arches.
It was as though I went not in the shade
That fell from walls and columns
With alternations of moonlight under the arches,
Passed by shadows cast from no bodies,
The sound of their steps like echoes of my own
And yet which moved as though they had once owned bodies.
Not in a night of sound and of the city's lights
But in a night without sound
In a flood of waters that had one sound and one motion
Continuously rising.
I strode on the pavement stones as through a flood
And knew the night as though it were a flood rising
Of immense disquietude. So many statues gone
That sat serene as these in the moonlit gardens
In brutal dissolution. As I said, these statues are old
And have the longing of stone
To become mere rocks. Brought into time
By the sculptor's delicate hand, these statues long
To return again to timelessness.
Cir. 1935

MYTHOLOGIES ON ARMCHAIRS

Such goddesses there were who strictly filled
The prim parlor: divinities not stone,
But half invisible amid mulberry silk,

Who sometimes stared, erect on armchairs,
Against a tawny velvet, among the tassels
And looped cords, while phantasmal fingers played
Upon a table of daguerreotypes
That fallen family's portrait; or taller stood
In the dim corner where the whatnot shelved
A maritime disorder: starfish, fossils, shells;
Thence with portentous voices, shrilling, dispelled
Illusions of the stereopticon.
Their talk was all of statues—soothing that stole
The fascinated ear of boyhood—hoopoes,
And such outlandish birds; a torn tongue
That silently wove itself in troubled threads;
Of faith's division and heaven overcome;
A divided house and all grandfathers dead.

Cir. 1938

MISTER PREVAL'S BALL

O! Mister Preval said I'll hire a hall
And 'vite all the niggers to a grand ball.
    Danse, O Calinda, boudoum, boudoum.

The hall turned out to be an old stable
An' supper laid on a long plank table.
                        Supper was laid
    Danse, O Calinda, boudoum, boudoum.

The mules in their stalls stood up and snorted
To see the way those darkies cavorted.
                    The way those crazy
                    darkies cavorted
    Danse, O Calinda, boudoum, boudoum.

There wasn't no light but the light o' the moon
Every darky came in paid a picayune.
    Danse, O Calinda, boudoum, boudoum.

For music Preval had an ol' banjo

bum banjo screeched

An' a fiddle that creaked like a dyin' crow.
   Danse, O Calinda, boudoum, boudoum.

His coat all grease an' his shirt all starch,
His one-eyed coachman led off the Grand
     March.

His ol' black blind

   Danse, O Calinda, boudoum, boudoum.

Old Nancy Latiche got the mostest laughs
When she lifted her skirt to show her false
     calves.
   Danse, O Calinda, boudoum, boudoum.

1936

"WE LINGERED IN THE PARLOR . . ."

We lingered in the parlor when the light was gone—
And last it left the bell-glass where it shone
Upon a mantel of white marble, between
Bronze candelabra, which so long upheld
Circles of crystals and their lights renewed,
Light after light, with glitter. And there were sprays
Confined in glass, like a retired delight,
'n memory only lovely, released beyond
 he condemnation of the accustomed world:
Wild flowers that were not flowers but wild shell
Imprisoned in shimmers like a losing wave's,
Petals of lucent yellow and pink rose,
Their branches pranked with conches as with buds.
As though some deluged life had been divulged
In words that scarcely spoke of love at all?
What quaint intention of the thought had found
That artifice of flowers to display

148

Spoils of a secret and crustaceous sea
And set them there in perfect clarity
Concealed, where none could touch, yet all could see?
The change of elements was too profound
To smile. We could but think what frantic patience
Had possessed those fingers to escape from summer
Before they came fastidiously on glass
As a transparent bound, and closed a space
Where the sea slept, could sleep the winds and the tides,
And where might sleep an immense misfortune.
We could not take our eyes away, nor move,
No more than if we'd seen a crime. None could
Withhold the dark. We sat and talked
Of trivial things until the moving darkness
Removed from sight the glass and from surmise
The unreal passions of another age.

Cir. 1938

PERCY SHELLEY

The question, lords and ladies, is
With what did Percy Shelley piss?
Was light dissolved in star showers thrown
When Percy Shelley had a bone?

Transcendental love we know
Is packed, but has no place to go.
And Percy's love, as he has said,
Resembled roses when they're dead.

And rose leaves when the rose is dead
Are out of place, like crumbs in bed.
No letter yet has come to light
To say if Percy rose at night.

149

No lady for whom Percy pined
Has left a diary behind;
And so there still remains a doubt
What Percy's love was all about.

Though scholars search, no letters come
Written in a flurry home;
We ask and ask, till silence palls,
Did Percy Bysshe have any balls?

1938

ART AND ACTION

Do what? Add my name to a Trotsky faction
To bury more revolutions?
Make integers of an improper fraction,
Distribute soup, or Salvation buns?
Assault the police in a fit of distraction,
From an office desk assail the Huns?
Declare the Black Shirt has a sexual attraction?
Rush over the border and rape some nuns?
Put on a medieval cataphraction,
Wear sandwich boards or collect old duns?
Study Karl Marx in a noted redaction
Or go lion hunting with seventeen guns,
Teach Henry Ford the oxcart's traction
Or follow Sir James and fly to new suns?
Present evils are for men of action,
Art has the irremediable ones.

Cir. 1939

CHOICE OF CROWNS

The wreath of desert thorn
Was given a last twist of scorn
And pressed upon the martyr's head
Until his patient forehead bled.

Laurel is the only wear
For it stays green in burning air
When cities cringing into dust
Clamor for a conqueror's lust.

Cir. 1939

MEANING OF A LION

The mighty lion on a rock
Stares at the desert and the sun
Immense burning in unison
Beneath his calm entrancèd look.

Tumultuous repose of beast
Aroused at night. His long tail slack
He leaps upon the desert's back
When hunger scents a starry east.

Erect descends a rocky slope
To slink uncolored through the brush;
Attains his herd: vaulting, to crush
A terror of wild antelope.

Aloud he shouts torment of must.
The lioness meets his roaring leap
Quivering: includes his clawing grip,
Tall curvet of immortal lust.

His rasping taste laps rottenness,
Returning to the zebra's hide.
All breathing life is mortified
Till age disjoints an ailing prowess.

Then jackals snarl about his corse,
Black vultures pick dead eyes from bone.

Secret in windy skeleton
The lion rots without remorse.

Cir. 1940

"LOOK AT THE COLUMNS . . ."

Look at the columns—how each stands alone
And all stand free! Ranged in a spacious order,
The trembling columns enclose a flight of time
That floods in the shafts with a following light,
Falters at the capitals and overflows
Intricately among the circling and encircled leaves,
That slowing motion being the acanthus' sleight.
Their prosody of silence stands in proof
Against the tongues of disputatious time.
Order is a changeling of the mind.
There's nothing lonelier than one column set
Against the casual clouds and changing sky.

Cir. 1940

NAUSET SANDS

I

Elude the dunes! By sunken pace
Through struggling sands,
Patched by the panting beach grass, come
To the long coast arrayed by sea-piled storms.

The north stands
Dissolute sands,
Sea-borne bulwarks against the sea.

South is an unlimited strand,
A waste of noon
Paced by no shadow.

And here the lonely man may stride
Unmeasured by the beach,
Strip, run and plunge
Through inborn sunburnt spray,
Then glistening stretch
Where in the destroying radiance
Of the aroused day
No shell survives. An imagined east
The sea! And all America is west!
And here at last a naked man may rest
Undaunted by the ancestral quest
As though it had not been,
In azure assumption of pure space
Untortured by the undaunted dream,
An hour stay, unshadowed of the sun,
And this the first as now the ultimate coast.

II

Domain that has no confines but in light,
Destroying space! Brute blue of noon now glared
Its death upon me. I saw them on their coast,
Their hearts as big with winds as though they had been sails,
And all their purpose prows turned into the sun.
Undream their doing. Lie down! Lie down!
The sea returns upon an instant and all their voyages
End at last in a bare body on the sand.
Into the world naked I came.
And now once more lie naked to the sky.*

---

* The manuscript of this poem contains a third section which is identical
with "The Statue of a Shadow." I conjecture that Bishop wrote "Nauset Sands"
before "The Statues"; suppressed all of "Nauset Sands" except part III,
which he included in "The Statues" as part V; then suppressed "The Statues,"
saving only "The Statue of a Shadow" as a single poem in Selected Poems.—
Editor.

THE STATUES

The Uneaten Gods

The clouds move, the sea returns
Bright beyond the radiance of summer islands,
White beyond blue inlets.
The sea is fair
Upon white crescents.
The sea is far
Casting gods in curds of white spray:
Bodies of gods, broken, the curled hair
Still bound at the temples; drowned gods,
Claspt by the shore, comely in seaweed lying,
The throats broken and silent.

The gods adorned the islands
Seasonable as summer
Or as clouds,
Sea-heights confusing cloud with spray.
The past is far,
That shore is far.
And even those upon the beach
Cannot eat the bodies of these gods:
The belly of the boy-god, like a lyre
Unstrung; the proud burden
Of the goddesses bowed
Stone, shadowing no soul upon the stone.
Even the poor upon that beach,
Prodding the sand, cannot eat
Fragments, shards, broken finds,
Unshadowed breasts and all
The secret shadowing of love upturned
Under the blue and brutal gaze of sky.

The sea returns upon the land—
Sea-lights suffusing all the shores
With dissolute silver—frothing, fades to sands.

This was the initial error, the fatal mischief
The bread broken, not the god
The bread eaten, no more the god
No more the being of the inconstant god
The wine drunk, the wine-vat drunken
An inebriation, not divine
The wine not blood, but only the grape's bleeding
The wine drunk, not the god's blood.
This was in truth the fatal error.
When food and drink are no more divine
Then they fail, they fail the body
Not the god fails, but wheatfield and vineyard
The god does not fail, for the god lives
When his body is drawn and broken.

The sea returns,
The coasts low-lying
And the sea hurrying
To close upon the land:
Concourse of confusion,
Incessant wavelets
Headlong clamoring,
Not with their own cries,
But with the harsh compulsion
Of the willing wind.

Only the waves are seen
Covetous of land,
Not the force under the waves,
Nor the forces above the waves,

Only the waves are seen
Spending
In one white dissolution of spray:
Sand withdrawn
Waste 'moil, and downward
Screeching of drowned shells.

Embodiments of time, the gods restored
Stars to the turning year; replaced the Pleiades,
And, summer's brilliant promise, hung
The Dog Star; sustained the shores with seasons
And seed of recollected harvests. Therefore, in
      love
With sun, the lovers clasped, the child was born,
Incarnate marvel of exhausted summer,
Cradled in straw. Imaginings of order
Rose, beyond the lucent headlands,
Above the marble stairs. And columns rose,
Voluptuous doves among the capitals,
Supporting roof and overcoming azure.
The gods stood. Men saw their simulacra
Display immortal visions. So let the wild
      white horses
Rise from the bay, and run, bestriding spindrift,
To rock the shores with stormier tramplings!
The gods stood. And while they stood, the state
And every sea-gaze circled to the same horizon,
All speech proclaimed one tongue of praise.

II

DUNES ON THE MARCH

Sands that array these shores
Into the silence of distances,
Trampling ranges of dunes:

Arrested now in ridges,
Rising, abandoned by the restless wind,
Ribbed by the storm, and bare, the sand
Is a dead saint's side. Speech is devoured
On the dry tongue,
Burning the vision
In excess of space.

Sprigged by a sparse grass,
Prickled by salt green, stretches the waste:
Sand, scattering glaucous moss,
Grey crop, crunching underfoot
In dryness.

So they appear shores
That are the desolate and abandoned sea!

III

Sojourn in the Desert

Pluck from the descent of glare,
The desert slope, the sprightly
Grasshopper! Let him perch
Suspiciously alive, upon a finger,
Stroke his wings, all summer
In the one bright eye!

Where should we find wild honey?
In this dry and torrid land
The grasshopper is the summer: summer
The grasshopper's springing,
Grating an age of silence to a winged sound.

Ascetic drought was there
Imposed by the sun,
A dry and diseased south,
Silence of sound;
But the saint's secret was not there
Not in the sand
The sand-bur, the yellow-flowered prickle.

In that dry and torrid land
Speech was devoured
On the hated tongue. Draining spittle
A taste of blood on the tongue,
We stood, or staggered toward the water-hole
Empty mirror of sun.

Amphion
Orpheus, the haggard John
In his wild cloak of camel's hair,
His legs gaunt and shaken,
His gaze bewildered,
Could not for all his meditation hear it.
It was not in the Wilderness.
John but heard the footsteps of Him who came,
John but heard the print of feet on sand,
Awfully approaching,
The Word in solitude approaching,
Far off, far, the feet barely posed
On the waiting desert.

Surviving shores
Of a sunken continent: sand and scrub-pine,
Scrub-oak and sand; the aromatic blaze
Of a blue noon warms the bay-leaf in the
          sea's sound.

Return of the Sea

Grateful the sound of the sea! Destruction cast
Upon the sterile shingle, grating the shores
In one white death of spray

Sounding

Return,
Return to darkness and the drowned
Oblivion of mounting tides that drench
The inward walls of caves! Convulsive flood
Rushing as though water were the word
Death made flesh
The Word death
And the Word made flesh!

Sounding

Look
Into the secret pools
Left on the rock by the refluent wave
And stirred by dimming water see
Your own remorseless face return
Among strange starfish and salt-oozing weed!

Sounding

Ships
There were once composed for commerce,
Bright shrouds, and prows that darkly clove
Oncoming crests while they pursued
Their gilded course toward the untrafficked
        isles.

Sounding

Swim
And let your naked breath expire
Under the overwhelming onslaught of the sea,
Or crook with counterstroke the coming wave
And rise, turned on a breath, and see
The sun in conscious triumph on the sky!

v

The Statue of Shadow *

This was that mystery of clearest light:
No cloud
No shadow of a cloud
Passed on the coast where then I stood.
A burning sand consumed my sight.
I saw my body cast
In shadow and was afraid.
I saw time vast
As my own shadow and was afraid.
Being both light and a vision of light,
I saw my stature cast.
The shade of all those centuries
Whose death is longing and fate a crime
Lay long
But no longer
Than the statue of shadow
The sun at its silent noon laid at my feet.

---

* This poem appears as a single poem in section III, from *Selected Poems*. I print both versions because they differ in several phrases. Which is the earlier cannot be definitely known at present; I surmise that the version here is the earlier, and that Bishop revised it as a separate poem, and decided at least temporarily not to publish "The Statues" as a sequence. "The Statues" was probably written in 1940. See note, p. 108.—*Editor*.

This was that mystery:
Time had no other feature.

THE GREAT STATUES

Since that I believe the high joy
Neither ascends nor descends
But simply burns
Brightness in the sense of silence
Being consumed in intelligence of beings.

Let us sustain the silence of great statues
Who stare out it seems in appalled serenity
It may be at nothing
As though there were nothing before them:
Stone eyes that foreknow a slowness of
    dissolution,
Stones crumbling in time; but only as seas
Dissolve strange outlines of coasts; overthrow
Citadels, sea-walls; rage wearing down rock
Ancient as the dawn; deliberate deluge of days
That rise and retract
In obedient disorder of tides and stars.

I have awakened from a dream of space!
Dunes on the march. I have come from a land
Of advancing deserts. Torrents of wings
Flow through the dust-hills there, timeless
    drone,
Settling with drought on devastation. They
    gaze at the sun there
Through a redness of dust-clouds. No saying
    of the Sun
That does not say, Cease, cease!

Let us stay by these ancient statues,
Flowing and naked, flower-crowned,
Attended in stone by dolphins and swans,
Reminding the gods were once beasts.
Let us stay by these antique statues,
For strange to relate it is only in arid
                    delays
That these stone mouths open
And the gods speak.

                    Not death
Is the last indignity of man, but an endless
Dying. Time lost, and centuries uncounted,
Violence reverberating under the arches,
The land dead and all wars disastrous.

It is fear that stands in these ancient statues,
The fear that life may cease.
It is only in fear that the gods speak.
That fear is upon us.

VII

THE ARCHIPELAGOES

I stood upon the seashore and looked over my
                    shoulder:
Upon this coast the silence of the stars
Is redeemed by another sapphire silence
Deepening in distance. The Cyprian star
Advances morning and restores the light.

These are my seas, my archipelagoes,
The sea crudded with foam, the white of wings
At dawn, the increasing lucent blue.

Far off, there roll on cloudless reefs
The formless origins of the sea.

The day returns, but not the day
Of these gods. Yet the dawn resumes the amazed
Smile of a brute Apollo,
Dazzling in bronze of sea-encrusted blue-green.
Past-destroying statue! Conquest of will
On an underworld of knowledge! Man knows
And knows he dies. And in this knowledge
Delight dwindles or like a flare increases.
Light dies and does not die: remains on stone.
All life begins in the refulgent body
And in the fault of love. Knowing begins
                with fear.

These are my seas, my archipelagoes,
The tides consenting to the cogent moon,
The islands where my will has peace
And temples erect their solitudes
Columns and white porches and aloft in stone
The eyeless statues of corrupted gods.
I have not heard the gods, but I have heard
The noise at dawn of doves among the capitals.
There have been sounds, too, at noon that would
                amaze you.

Noon at its height: but not the noon of these gods,
Light conceived as stone. The day
Of these gods is descended
Into solid bodies on the beach,
With the sun burning, darkened
And burning with blood. The laughter-running boys
Leap, and maintain their increase in the air.

I was twice born,
Once begotten by my father,
Once by the divine Sun,
My will consenting to that Word whose will
Ordains the copulations and the putrefactions,
The seed dying that love may not die,
The death of seed that the body may not die,
Corruption of the body that the land may not perish.

Circlets of foam from the formless sea
The seacrests wreathing all the shores with
        spray
Dissolving into light, light into spray,
Fast fading, fast falling, fading.

The time-adorning monuments
Restore the secrets of eternity.

Cir. 1940

EXPERIENCE OF THE DESERT *

Ascetic drought was there, silence of sun,
But the secret was not there,
Not in the sand, the sand-bur,
Not in the disappearing sun
When the last light left the yellow-flowered prickle

And night-dew fell. In that dry and torrid land
Speech was devoured
On the dry tongue. The throat
Drained spittle, gulping its own moisture.
We drew to the water-holes, empty mirrors of sun.

---

  * This poem is evidently an early draft of "Sojourn in the Desert," section III
of "The Statues."

There like the tumultuous Anthony
We drank, we too drank stale.
But the puddled piss no savor stole
From a soldier's helmet.
Unused our valor and unasked in action.

Then like that other, the demoniac, Anthony
We clothed the demented skeleton
No more in flesh but fire. It blamed and shamed
And burned, but could not hide mortality.
Contemplation could not save us who saw no conquest.

Cir. 1940

STATUE ON THE SQUARE

History is a monument, on which
It is possible with delay to decipher
Some counsels for conduct, a few precepts,
All difficult to apply. For, aside
From the inane flattery of the words,
Life demands an interim between the letters
To breathe, to love, to contemplate in action
The worth of these inscriptions. Then, too,
The carving is subject much to age's
Confusions, being scratched with interlinears
Of contempt, as well as the corruptions
Of decay. Above, of course, is the hero,
A conqueror who wears his wig in clouds;
Though marred by defecations of the pigeons
Arrogant in the gaze, and slightly turned
As though in expectation of all praise;
Exhaling pride in stone. His being moulds
To its own motion a marble armor
For sheer magnificence worn and overlaid
With minute goats, nereids in wreaths,

165

And a rare likeness of the sun-god;
A simulacrum, say, of Roman crime,
This late inheritor of civil conquest.
Stay against anarchy, terror smiles as law.
Below, then, is the recently repaved square,
The old cobbles having been removed
After repeated insurrections, when the stones,
Hurtled as weapons, piled in barricades,
Stopped the charge converging on the crowd
Of the craven cavalry. Indeed, the square has seen
Riots of starvelings, executions of nobles,
And at times massacres of everybody.
The record is certainly one of oppression.
But then I never imagined myself a ruler
Or supposed in my arm capacity to destroy
A state corrupt to anguish, build a better.
This much, however, seems to me evident:
A classless state demands a dictator,
With you and me as nothing, that He may be all:
Justinian, Napoleon, Stalin.
I have enough, things being as they are,
A little longer to dispose with honor
This small domain, this island which I own,
This body; and ask but calmly to observe,
Even as in the greater state, decay,
Being careful to consider for both an end,
A fate seen with displeasure, not with fear.

Cir. 1940

CAPE COD GRAVES

Sea dunes, sand waves
That shape the shudder of the winds,
These are the true accumulations,
As the sea, that old trickster, is the true grave.

166

Look at the tumbling stones on the old mounds!
Titles to graves. Each has a name.
But go down into the ground,
Deep, deep, deep. The sea has the bones.

At seadawn the surge sang
And all day the sea brought what day sought.
At dusk the sea surged. And the sea sang
A doom's dream of drowned men's bones.

Scrub pine, sand pine,
Twisted by the gale's tang, tough
In a cloud, elude no storm. Pines hold
The harried hollows behind the dunes.

Standing at land's end, these are the trees,
These are the trees to look upon,
And the sea, the sea, that receives a man
And with one wave washes away the name.

The grave is not a door through which to escape
The body of this death
When bare age has scraped all memory from bone.
The grave is a squall.

When song surged, the sea sang
Its own change. Hungry for land,
Hastening spawn, distributing wrack,
The sea's sound was a joy of fear.

Cir. 1942

WRITTEN FOR RICHARD C. POWELL, TO AMUSE, SUMMER 1943 *

Few men, dear Dick, could be much needier
Than I of your Encyclopaedia.

---

* So far as can be known at present, this is the last verse that Bishop wrote except his own epitaph. See my Memoir, p. xvi.—*Editor.*

You know what pleasure I derive
From seeing plants remain alive,
And how I scatter Vigoro
And water them to make them grow.
If I've succeeded, credit chance,
And when I've failed, blame ignorance.
But now no more I'm at the mercy
Of casual luck or William Hersey,
Nor need I ever be distracted
And wonder how I should have acted.
I have your book. There I'll repair
All that was lacking in my care.
I turn its pages and I find
So much I never brought to mind,
Learning at last what measures will do
To overcome the downy mildew,
And how to poison every beetle
That comes from Popocatepetl.
Henceforth I shall not falter, but
Go armed to deal with thrips and smut.
For O, I learn that never ease is
For the gardener while diseases
(Not to speak of other things
That climb and crawl and come on wings)
Lie in wait for all he's planted.
Sprays, it seems, must not be scanted
While there wait stunt, scale, chlorosis,
Or aphids with their green probosces.
Yet leaf by leaf still curls, decays
Unless you dust, between the sprays,
Sulphur after nicotine
For pests too tiny to be seen,
Such as microscopic mite
Who lives at all times out of sight
Yet whose effects can be discerned

By what they've blistered, browned and burned.
I sometimes wonder that a flower
Dares to survive a single hour
Unassisted by such lore
As that on which I now may pore;
For now I know one can combat
That with this and this with that,
And even find the skill to fight
Phythophthora and Bortrytis blight,
And other things of worse repute
Attacking flower and leaf and fruit.

So now I dream of what I'll grow
When spring comes after frost and snow:
Hackamatack and Halesia,
Holodiscus and Nemesia,
Blessed Thistle, Holy Grass,
Bunya Bunya, Eriobotryas,
Nelumbium and Prickly Pear,
And other species just as rare.
And if success attends my labor
I'll thank again my kindly neighbor,
Who also wields a wicked trowel—
I mean my good friend, Richard Powell.

1943

TRANSLATIONS

TRANSLATIONS

FROM THE GREEK ANTHOLOGY

I

EPITAPH

Stranger who stayest by this stone
Find no fault, for I find none
And I lie dead in the dark alone.

1933

II

TO A SWALLOW

Relish honey. If you please
Regale yourself on Attic bees.
But spare, O airy chatterer,
Spare the chattering grasshopper!

Winging, spare his gilded wings,
Chatterer, his chatterings.
Summer's child, do not molest
Him the summer's humblest guest.

Note: The three translations from the Greek anthology, "Ieu M'Escondisc,"
"Quan Lo Rius La Fontana," "Venus Anadyomene," and "Loin des Oiseaux"
made up section IV of *Now With His Love*. All of Bishop's verse translations
appear in this section of *Collected Poems.—Editor.*

Snatch not for your hungry young
One who like yourself has sung—
For it is neither just nor fit
That poets should each other eat.

1930

III
OFFERINGS

To the Paphian, these roses traced
With silver dew I bear;
To Artemis this girdle from my waist;
To Pallas this brief tress of hair;

Remembering their favors: I who drew
My lover to my bed and was undone
By love. To him I have been true
And three times heard him cry, "A son!"

1933

IEU M'ESCONDISC, DOMPNA, QUE MAL NON MIER

From the Provençal of Bertran de Born

O let me, Lady, silence calumny
And end these lies envy has laid on me.
In God's name, I pray you! Let them not confuse
Your heart that is all faith and courtesy,
Complaisance, truth and tender loyalty,
However they assail me with abuse.

At first cast may I lose my hawk in air,
See falcons strike it at my wrist and tear
It from me, to pluck it to the bloodied bone,
If ever the love I have of you could bear
I look upon another with desire to share
That bed whereon I get no rest alone.

And now that I may utterly disencumber
My course from shame the protest shall be sombre:
If ever I have failed toward you in thought
When we shall be alone in the high chamber
May my powers fail and my heart not remember
To send blood into my veins for the bout.

If I sit down to tables may my luck
Change so I cannot win by hook or crook;
When I start gaming may the dice conspire
Always to fall upon the lowest stroke;
If ever I sought another and forsook
You whom alone I love, alone desire.

May I share Altafort with other lords
And in the tower may we be four swords
And no love lost among the lot. But rather
May I go always covered round with guards
Crossbowmen, leeches, sergeants and gatewards,
If ever I had heart to love another.

O Lady, leave me for another knight
Nor let me know where to avenge the slight;
May the winds fail me when beyond the sea,
And the King's porters drub me from his sight;
In press of battle may I take first flight,
If they lie not who tell these tales of me.

Lady, I have a goshawk, finely mewed,
Swift to the wild duck, trained and unsubdued
By any bird that flies, heron or swan
Or even the black eagle, and I would
Gladly for your sake see her droop immewed,
Sullen and slow to fly, fat as a capon.

Envious liars, feinting with calumny,
Since through my lady you have troubled me,
You were advised to leave me well alone.

1933

QUAN LO RIUS DE LA FONTANA

From the Provençal Jaufre Rudel, Prince of Blaia

When the thin fountains are again
Clear streams and sunlight interfused,
When flower of the wild rose is seen,
And nightingales upon the bough
Smooth and renew with charged refrain
Their sweet songs, I too must begin
Sweetly to rearrange my own.

Love of a faraway domain,
For your sake all my heart is bruised
And for my hurt no medicine
Is found—unless it were that now
I might to the high bride bed attain
And under the curtains enter in
To the desired companion.

But since there's nothing I can win
Marvel not I am brought low.
No Christian of nobler strain
Ever was, and God has refused
Rivalry to the Sarrazin.
He has drunk well of honey-rain
That's had her breast to lie upon.

Endless desire of her's within
My heart, which cannot but avow
That it is coiled in a rich skein
And covetously is abused.

My grief is as the thorn's prick keen
But joy has so appeased my pain
I want no man's compassion.

Unscrivened on dry parchment skin
I send the song, singing the low
Sounds of Provence, that it obtain
Sir Hugo Brun. Since I am used
To hear him praised of the Poitevin
And through all Brittany and Maine
Filhol shall sing to him alone.

1933

VENUS ANADYOMENE

From the French of Arthur Rimbaud

As from a coffin of green zinc, a skull
Of woman's hair, brown, larded with pomade
From an old bathtub rises, slow and dull,
Patched with repairs were better never made,

Then the grey, greasy neck, broad shoulder blade
And back too short that caving in sticks out.
The fat beneath the skin's in layers laid,
The rolling sides have put all shape to rout.

The backbone's rather red; and the whole smell
Is horribly strange. More than one odd lump
Deserves a stooping lens to be seen well.

Two words inscribe the loins: *Clara Venus.*
—The whole bulk moves and spreading its big rump
Bares, hideously beautiful, an ulcered anus.

1933

177

LOIN DES OISEAUX, DES TROUPEAUX, DES VILLAGEOISES

From the French of Arthur Rimbaud

Far from the birds, the herds, the village girls
What did I drink, in heather to my knees,
Within a tender grove of walnut trees
In the warm green mist of an afternoon?

What could I drink in that young stream,
—Tuneless reeds, flowerless grass, cloudy sky!—
Drink from those yellow gourds, far from the dreamed of
Hut? Gold that drunk brought sweat to the skin.

I might have swayed a queer sign for an inn.
—A long wind swept the clouds away. That night
The waters of the wood were sunk in sands
And a wind from God flung glass on all the ponds.

Weeping, I saw the gold,—and could not drink.

1933

QUID FACTUM EST, QUOD TU PROIECTIS, IUPPITER, ARMIS

From the Latin of Petronius Arbiter

Can it indeed be, Jove, you have grown old?
Now if ever were the moment to put on
Brute forehead and the bull's horns, or unfold
The outrageous beauty of a busking swan.

This is only Danaë. Desire
To touch her body where she lies—and all
That once was god, involved in such a fire,
Must change to fame and as a gold rain fall.

1941

THE PEASANT DECLARES HIS LOVE

From the French of Emile Roumer

High-yellow of my heart, with breasts like tangerines,
you taste better to me than eggplant stuffed with crab,
you are the tripe in my pepper-pot,
the dumpling in my peas, my tea of aromatic herbs.
You are the corned beef whose customhouse is my heart,
my mush with syrup that trickles down the throat.
You are a steaming dish, mushroom cooked with rice,
crisp potato fries, and little fish fried brown . . .
My hankering for love follows you wherever you go.
Your bum is a gorgeous basket brimming with fruits and
    meat.

1942

THEN TWIST THE NECK OF THIS
DELUSIVE SWAN

From the Spanish of Enrique González Martínez

Then twist the neck of this delusive swan,
white stress upon the fountain's overflow,
that merely drifts in grace and cannot know
the reed's green soul and the mute cry of stone.

Avoid all form, all speech, that does not go
shifting its beat in secret unison
with life. . . . Love life to adoration!
Let life accept the homage you bestow.

See how the sapient owl, winging the gap
from high Olympus, even from Pallas' lap,
closes upon this tree its noiseless flight . . .

179

Here is no swan's grace. But an unquiet stare
interprets through the penetrable air
the inscrutable volume of the silent night.

1942

PEASANT VICTORY

From the Spanish of Mariano G. Fernandez

The countryside poured on the roads
Mustered its droves, men dumbed with anger.
For the wind had brought them
Bad news out of Spain:

The Carlists are coming!

One like the rest.
Out of the fields, Sylvester,
Stood and harangued them:
—The Carlists, he shouted,
Are coming this way!
The Carlists are coming
Once more to shoot us
Down in our furrows,
To lay waste and to pillage
This land that is ours, and still
Our hope and always our sorrow.
The Carlists—you know them!—
Are still sore
With that old wound
Our grandfathers gave them.
They are marching against us
And all that is ours.
Our wives and our children
Are no longer ours. They are war's booty
And wait the Carlists.

Nothing will save them!
—Scythes, said a countryman
Slyly and quietly,
That used to stop them.

—But what good are scythes
When bullets are quicker?
In his whole soul
Sylvester was afflicted.
Shouts in the streets,
Then from the alleys the sound
Of running and the first volleys.
The Fascists in the town
Were alarmed and arming.

Then the same countryman
Spoke, quietly, boldly:
—What do we do now, Captain?
And Sylvester told him.

Only at the manor of the marquess
Hope to obtain arms for our hands.
It is we now who are the noble warriors,
Our hands committed to the noblest purpose:
To defend our wives
To hold our homes
To cherish our children—
When ever had war a nobler aim?

The moon was down. Night slouched
In the streets, stood in the doorways. Dawn
Already peering from rooftops
Saw its own pallor on windows.
It is a long way to the marquess's,
Twelve miles marching by the road.

But birds must as peasants do
Wake before the light. And the birds sang.

Ah, how their shouts rang,
How the sun rose in the peasants' eyes!

—All I want is my pick of the rifles.
—If I once get my hands on the hunting
Racks! —Give me a pistol!

River, mountain, mill,
All were left behind their shoulders.

It is a long way to the marquess's,
Twelve miles marching by the road.

Without resistance, without a struggle,
The peasants seized their arms,
Which at once all burst
Under their fingers
To a bloom of bullets.
They felt so good-hearted
They spared the marchioness.
They felt so light-hearted
They left their lives to the cowering maidservants.
The men were long gone
To the ranks of the Carlists.
And with one voice, the peasants
Cried, what a pity!
And back through the fields
They marched with their weapons
Jogging a joyous
Dance on their shoulders.

Justice out of heaven
Was now descending. Through long nights

Prayed for, justice was come down
To earth from heaven. They marched through the fields.
And the stones and the trees,
And the flocks by the streams in pastures,
And the staring herds and the plowed lands,
All lived in another light,
All received light from the armed and marching peasants.
And they looked at one another
Strangely, as men look on one long lost
And, after hope has long been lost, recovered.

The village was ready for them,
When their rifles spoke
With the tongues of freedom.
Fighting was brief, the battle
Measured by the murders to be done:
The mayor, paid off for his usury,
Ripped through those bowels
Where mercy was not; the guards
In their cocked hats, complacently
Shot down, to the last
Obedient to their civic orders;
Four or five rich men
Who had called themselves Fascists;
The barricaded priest
And that old trollop he called his maid.
When it was all over and the village
Helped from a bad heredity,
The peasants came together
In the open square
To hear Sylvester, their captain.

—What now, Sylvester? —What do we do?

—Listen, my friends,
They are many, we are few.

Our war is over, our little battle,
But a bigger battle rages in Spain,
A longer war. There our hopes call us.
Turn out your cattle
To feed in the pastures;
Find some safe
Refuge for your families;
Store our records. Then we will go
To take our places in the Spanish dance.
On the other side of the mountains
There are comrades. The workers
Have pulled their belts tighter
And are singing their hopes
Of all that will follow
The horror of battle,
The carnage and conquest,
When peace brings its calm.

1937

EARLY POEMS

UNCOLLECTED EARLY POEMS
1912-1917

UNCOLLECTED EARLY POEMS

TO A WOODLAND POOL *

Clear placid pool, inclosed by forests dank,
    Like one fair pearl enclasped by emeralds green,
How sweet it is upon thy mossy bank
    To lie and gaze upon thy deep serene,
Which, like some rare old tapestry, hath been
    Embroidered by the deftly fingered Sun
With leafy trees in vert and sapphire done,
    Flowers, and rifts of azure sky between!
Here would I gladly lie the livelong day
    And hear no creature save the wood peewee,
Her soul outpouring in some tear-filled lay
    Or the soft droning of the homing bee;
For here doth matchless beauty hold full sway
    And fill the soul with sweetest harmony.

1912

EXPERIMENTS IN CLASSIC METRES

I. UPON A LIST OF NAMES OF THE HEROINES OF THE OLD FRENCH ROMANCES

(*Alcaics*)

Names, sweet as sleep shed softly on slumberous
Eyelids, of queens long dead and ensepulchred,
    Who once by lone sea-casements sorrowed,
        Hearing the perilous seas beneath them;

---

* This is probably Bishop's first published poem.—*Editor.*

And leaning forth, saw reaches mysterious,
Highways of moonlight, endlessly glimmering,
    Saw too the sweet, still stars and trembled,
      Knowing again the unuttered longing;

Or haply, night-long sleeplessly pondering,
Wrought sweetest music out of their loneliness,
    With skill to mate each word with lute-strings
      Wondrously smitten to dulcet quirings:

Names lost in dust now, save when some yellowing
Moth-shredded parchment, stirred from oblivion,
    Yields once again names such as these names,
      Sweeter than light to an Eastern diver.

II. To Catullus

(Hendecasyllabics)

Once before the unspeeding feet o'ertake me,
Once before the alluring arms enfold me,
Or the finger of silence seals my eyelids,
Stands my hope to behold thy haunt, Catullus,
        Sirmio, which nor earth nor water
Ever utterly yields, but ever sunlight
Wakes on showering flights of foam, and foam-lights
All night fall on enchanted shores save only
Where the land with reluctant hope retains them.
So, once, Death in the midst of song set round thee
Streams impassable, girt with barren rushes,
Vain of bloom or of any earthly fruitage,
Steeped in tears as in dew and watched by dead men.
Yet still Life with reluctance gazes after,
Holds thy songs to her heart and haply weeping
Shades her tears with the light of laughing eyelids;

Half smiles, knowing not all of thee can perish,
Half smiles, knowing that neither Death nor Silence,
Time, nor ruinous season shod with hoar-frost,
Vexed with ravening teeth of winds and hail-blight,
Change, nor shadowy touch of halt Oblivion
Dares dissever thy songs from her forever.

1916

THE GREAT HATER

*A Proposed Companion Piece to Rupert Brooke's
"The Great Lover"*

I have been so great a hater: found my days
Filled full of things deserving hate's high praise
And homage. Oh, I that have learned to hate
Shall never want for pleasure; soon or late,
I'll find things hateful while I have my breath.
And when I die, I'll bite my thumb at Death.
But that's anon. I now must set you down
Things that I have hated:

                              A certain shade of brown
Which elder ladies love; wet roofs that drip
Their huge drops on your neck; short sheets that slip
And leave your ankles freezing; fires that smoke;
Carved, heavy furniture of varnished oak;
The food of farmers, and their stupid talk;
The feel of live wet fur; the shriek of chalk;
The hum of Autumn's gnats; smell of closed rooms,
And the rank breath of heavy dahlia blooms
Kept three days longer than they should have been;
White cups and plates, almost but not quite clean;
Lust in old men, coldness in the young;
Cheap love-songs and the tunes to which they're sung;

White moths which feast through long autumnal eves
In chests and closets; books with uncut leaves;
The hour of waking; late-seen gibbous moons;
And sugar in which dull people thrust wet spoons;
The loneliness of crowds, and the warm fret
Of April nights when the fresh grasses set
Youth and desire, night and still sleep at strife . . .
Death I have hated and, sometimes, even Life.

All these which I have known, kept, hated well,
I would set down, unchanged, unchangeable,
Against that hour when I shall lightly run
Along the windy pathways of the sun,
A strangely free and unannoyed ghost,
And start and turn and, finding I have lost
All these my treasured hatreds, bow my head
And tremble, knowing at length that I am dead.

1916 *

. . . WE SHALL NOT KNOW NEXT APRIL

Princeton: Class Poem, 1917

The Spring comes down this way again
With footsteps like the fall of rain,
And garments changing like a mist
From sudden gold to amethyst.
She's taken to the road that wanders down
From Kensington to Morristown;
At Torresdale none saw her pass,
But oh, her footprint on the grass!
They say she'd scarcely smile in Trenton
But a little by each bole she'd leant on
Began to stir with tiny green;

---

* Reprinted in *Vanity Fair*, April 1920; the later version is printed here.—
Editor.

And you can see that she has been
By Stony Brook, for through the mold
The heart-shaped violet leaves unfold,
And blades of white and violet
Show wherever her feet were set.

But Princeton is the place of places
Where first she lingers in her traces.
Flowers are many and grass is deep,
And all the ways are calm as sleep
And rich as a dream. There she stays
And half forgets to count her days.
Oh! Spring comes down these ways once more
Turning the wards on a precious store
Of balm and saffron, myrrh and nard,
Whose scent is spilt on every sward,
As once in Bethany they poured
A costly spice before our Lord.

But what of all the Princeton men
Who shall not come these ways again,
Or if they come, then not together
As in the old triumphant weather
When it was wealth but to behold
The blue sky fade to a sky of gold,
Then deepen to a richer blue
With points of gold just pricking through?
Oh! what of all the Princeton men
Who shall not know next April when
These elms and maples blend their shade,
And colors change, and the grass is laid
With snow-white petals instead of snow?
For Princeton men of all I know
Love best the way that leaves a friend
A trust to hold by to the end.

For Princeton men of all the earth
Know best the quiet ways of mirth.
They are not over good, nor yet
Dark with the things the good regret.
They never rise before the dawn
Or linger after midnight's gone,
Straining with curious brain and eyes
To grow inordinately wise.
But oh! the one essential truth,
The ancient carelessness of youth—
That holds life all but cheap unless
Wisdom is touched with kindliness.
For them there is one word—Farewell,
And after, silence.

            Who can tell
Which shall achieve a heritage
Of quiet eyes and serene age
And come again and find these places
Fair with light of ghostly faces,
And try these walks till memory
Comes sweet as hidden harmony?
Or who shall lie ungarlanded
Where France lays dust upon her dead,
All thought laid by, their youth foregone,
Glad at the last, if but the dawn
Follow where night shows fugitive?
Such gifts as these no god could give,
And they fare well.

            And what of her,
Now, then, and still our nurturer,
Our Lady of the Courts and Spires,
Crowned with the seven mystic fires,
The Three and Four which scholars hold
Of purer worth than sea-born gold.

There is no word a son can say
But wish her men like these alway.
For she—her ways are not as ours,
She sits above the tide of hours,
Life, death may take her sons, but she
Sits throned in that eternity
Where Love and Truth and Beauty are
Of lordlier brilliance than a star.

1917

"THEY SHOULD HAVE GONE FORTH WITH BANNERS"

They should have gone forth with banners,
With the sounding and resounding of many trumpets,
Then, in the midst thereof,
Her terrible head bound with laurels and gold,
Victory, her broad wings
Fanning the air with a light and rumor of gold,
Her bloody feet leaving their stain on the highway
And her high sword pointing the way they were to go.

But they went forth silently,
With heads bowed,
With backs bent under strong burdens
And a fitful smile of pity on their closed lips,
Seeing how little a thing it is to die.

1917

THE HUNCHBACK

I saw a hunchback climb over a hill
Carrying slops for the pigs to swill.

The snow was hard, the air was frore,
As he cast a bluish shadow before.

Over the frozen hills he came
Like one who is neither strong nor lame,

And I saw his face as he passed me by,
And the hateful look of his dead-fish eye,

His face like the face of a wrinkled child
Who has never laughed or played or smiled.

I watched him till his work was done,
And suddenly God went out of the sun,

Went out of the sun without a sound;
But the great pigs trampling the frozen ground.

The hunchback turned and retracked the snows,
But where God's gone, there's no man knows.

1919 *

* Reprinted in *Poetry: A Magazine of Verse*, June 1921.—*Editor.*

GREEN FRUIT

1917

GREEN FRUIT

FABRICS AND SOULS
THE NASSAU INN

Night and rain—a silver grating on the night;
  Rain, and the wet leaves sobbing beneath my feet;
The small inn waits across the sodden leaves,
Silence at its doors and darkness in the eaves.

The iron lanterns, aureoled with light,
  Smear the wet pavements with gold and the wet street
With silver: you would say that fold on fold
Night was being unravelled into gold.

Midnight, deadened like repeated rhyme,
  Sounds from the old North . . . I were best in bed.
It's a cold drizzle . . . and the soundless dead
Go groping past and melt into the inn.

Here comes the fops and gallants of old time
  In the great morning of the Rights of Man,
Black redingotes and white curled collars to the chin,
The bronze hair tossed in a style republican,

Or in the manner of the Corporal
  Who fed men's hearts with fire from Italy,
Stringy and black, smeared with *huile antique*
To lie like a spaniel's ears along the cheek.

Huge shadows wavered over the rough wall;
   Rich firelight swam into the wine to die;
With snaps of silver the glasses shone and touched,
Freedom was thundered, lyric passion smutched.

Here I should have come under a black cape,
   A gold silk waistcoat winking in the folds,
And slipping into the quietest of seats
Unpocketed in boards of drab—John Keats.

Then, letting the black edge of my mantle drape
   Over one arm—while silver tapped with snuff—
Crumpling my brows as when a grandan scolds,
Read silently each page and sneezed, "What stuff!"

Oh, they were brave lads and they bravely dreamed,—
   What matter if they drank and gamed and died?
They dared to dream that man might still be free,
And pledged in bitter claret—Liberty.

And me on whom that heavenly dawn has gleamed
   As sunset only—me they hail in pride,
Brother, whenever the rain's slow parallels meet
In shining pallors through the shadowy street.

1917

MISS ELLEN

If any guest comes in to tea
   Miss Ellen's gay as one could hope.
She sits and knits incessantly
   Yellow and white or heliotrope.
She says,—"This happened yesterday,"
   Or, "How the days are growing short,
It's scarcely five, and the sky's gray,"
     "But then, of course, she's not our sort."

Then tea comes in with squares of toast,
    Dusted with sweetened cinnamon,
And cakes which are Miss Ellen's boast
    Whenever cakes are touched upon.
With sprightly grace she brews her tea
    And fills each cup with amber light
And fragrant warmth. Then first you see
    How thin her face is, and how white
The broken shadows of her hair,
    And from her eyes guess what regret
Is master of that gracious air.
    But then she smiles—and you forget.
And if you stay to chat a bit
    You'll find her gay as one could hope;
Like silver flies the needles flit
    Through yellow, white and heliotrope.
But when the room's a violet dusk,
    And all the ghostly candles stir
Their airy fingers, hints of musk
    Mingle with long-dried lavender.
For then Miss Ellen's knees are weighed
    With a box of dark, rich-scented wood,
Where youth and vanity are laid
    With all whose beauty has withstood
Miss Ellen's fading suns and snows:
    Carven marvels of ivory,
Yellowing laces, ruined rose,
    And fans that are filmy coquetry.
Then sometimes with a quiet grace
    She'll smile at the air where nothing is,
And spreading her fan's stiff pattern lace,
    Lift her hand for a phantom kiss.
And then again till late at night,
    She'll sit and stare with vacant eyes
Where youth and beauty and delight
    Lie hid in their scented secrecies.

BOUDOIR

The place still speaks of the worn-out beauty of roses,
  And half retrieves a failure of bergamote;
Rich light—and a silence so rich one all but supposes
  The voice of the clavichord stirs to a dead gavotte.

For the light grows soft, and the silence forever quavers,
  As if it would fail in a measure of satin and lace,
Some eighteenth-century madness that sighs and wavers
  From a life exquisitely vain to a dying grace.

This was the music she loved; we heard her often,
  Walking there in the green-clipt garden plots outside.
It was just at the time when the summer begins to soften,
  And cicadas are shrill in the long afternoon, that she died.

The gaudy macaw still climbs in the folds of the curtain;
  The chintz flowers fade where the late sun strikes them aslant.
Here are her books, too: Pope and the earlier Burton,
  A worn Verlaine—*Bonheur* and the *Fêtes Galantes*.

Come, let us go. I am done. Here one recovers
  So much of the past, yet fails at the last to find
Aught that made it the season of loves and lovers.
  Give me your hand. She was lovely. Mine eyes blind.

PLATO IN ITALY

An alley of dark cypresses
Hides an enrondured pool of light;
And there the young musicians come
With instruments for her delight.
Silk-clad, their brown cropped locks are bowed
Over dim lutes that sigh aloud;
Or else with heads thrown back they tease
Reverberate echoes from the drum.

The stiff folds of her rich brocade
Crush with faint sound the first dead leaves,
As her page lets slips the lustrous train.
Her eyes are sad, and her bosom heaves;
For the poet walking with her lays bare
That Love which moves the starrier air,
The heavenly love, and its earthly shade—
On earth the lovelier of the twain.

INTERIOR

The divine languor of souls beyond surprise
Lives in the cold curve of her lip; her eyes
Are calm as with a deep desire foregone.
Her jewelled ears drip threaded pearls upon
The fragile laces of her flaring ruff;
Her bosom sighs in crimson, and a rich stuff·
Tumbles in crimson folds about her feet.

With shrivelled shanks crossed on a cushioned seat,
A cloaked and ruffled dwarf strums on a lute;
His head is small and wrinkled like a fruit
Rotten at heart and ripe before its time.
Always from his plaited ruffles croaks a rhyme
To match the tremor of the shaken strings.

She hears the lute's false music, but it brings
No word; she sees the dwarf, but far away.
Sometimes a feathered fan of Africa
Taps a dull measure on her finger tips,
And again a pungent phial meets her lips
And pauses. A sound of heels—and she has guessed
Black beard, lank cheeks, chill hands, and all the rest,
And, lowering the flask without a word,
She turns with perfect calm to greet her lord.

FILIPPO'S WIFE

A serving woman speaks:

Black velvet trails its folds over the day;
White tapers dripping in their silver frames
Wave their thin flames and shadows in the wind.

Pia, Pompia, Bella Cunizza, come—come away!

We will not touch her till the end of day.
Her cheeks are clear as tapers tipped with flames,
Her lips like red leaves frightened in the wind.

Pia, Pompia, Bella Cunizza, come—come away!

Her toes are stiffened like a stork's in flight.
She's laid upon her bed, on the white sheets,
Her hands pressed on her smooth bust like a saint.

Pia, Pompia, come into the light.

When first we found her, her dead lips were white,
Then Ser Filippo found her straightened on her sheets.
There are shrewd poisons shut in scarlet paint.

Bella Cunizza, come into the light.

Sh-h! There slides in black doublet and black hose,
White cheeks against black velvet, lips that move,
And living lips that kiss the painted mouth!

I begin to be afraid, Pia, keep close.

White petals meddling with the red-drenched rose. . . .
When you are alive—that is the time for love,
And sobbing palm on hand and mouth on mouth.

Bella Cunizza, pinch the arras close.

There is a tottering and grasping and straying of hands,
And a dull sound—ho!—like a headsman's thud,
When the cut head swims all oozy from the axe.

A flare of scarlet with black velvet bands!

Pietro's hands parry for our lady's hands.
His lips were pale, and now—is it blood?
His eyes strain upward, open; the thighs relax.

Take care, lest Filippo see you where he stands!

GOSSIP

Rime riche

If Cecco'd stay at home and not be seen
   He'd hear such things as no man wants to see;
For soon as Messer Sposo's off the scene,
   They say Fra Gian forgets his future see,
While he and Cecco's wife as one adore
   Some common saint. Now no one surely knows
If't be Saint Venus of the Bolted Door,
   But gossip wags it so with "ayes" and "noes."
I'm not the one to say if such things be,
   But Mona Giulia might be watched a bit,
And one might hint, "Cecco, a great black bee
   Sips at your honey," or "Another's bit
Your topmost apple." It's always well
To see no poisoner lurks about one's well.

MESSALINA PREPARES A FESTIVAL

I am the queen of Italy.
These were the signs God set on me;
A barren beauty subtle and sleek,
Curled carven hair, and cheeks worn wan
With fierce false lips of many a man.
—Swinburne.

I

Claudius

"The great image of authority"

A naked negress, flanked in folds of blue,
Stands motionless, her brown skin edged with blue
Where silk crumples its last folds on the floor.
Her silver sandals startle the dull floor
With sudden light. Chased silver weighs her hands
With a square coffer, into which white hands
Stray for smooth ointments. The air is full of breath,
And the still chamber sighs and waits for death.
A huge bulk, yellow-bellied like a gourd,
Writhes on the bed. The bloated lids are lowered
Over the wine-veined eyes. The white hands stray
Toward the white ointment. New wavers stray
Through the blue silk as the blue shadows part.
White limbs. A peacock feather, irised at heart,
Tickles the yellow layers of the thick neck—
And Rome is saved from universal wreck!
The naked negress, flanked in folds of blue,
Stands motionless, her brown skin edged with blue.
Her breasts are pointed, heavy. Her thick lips
Curl outward like a trumpet-flower's tips.

MORNING

Three old women scrub the marble floor,
Three old women whose knees crunch on the floor,
Circle and swish and dip their rags,
And scrub again. Three gray hags:
One with her cheeks all fallen in
Where toothless gums suck at the skin;
The lashes are gone from her rheumy eyes;
And one whose bony shoulders rise
To a peaked hump behind her head;
And one whose eyes are teary and red,
With a wrinkled mass beneath each eye,
Like a scrubbing cloth that's been wrung dry.
Three old women scrubbing the rose-strewn floor,
Three old women whose knees ache at the hard floor.

SONNET

Sleep brought me vision of my lady dead,
   Robed as of old time in a silken gown,
With violets clustered round her perfect head,
   And violets gathered where her robe fell down
   Even to where her silken shoes were sewn
With dust of silver and stained purple thread;
   Her vesture's dyes were something fainter grown;
And the dusk buds held memory of scents shed.

But in her face there seemed a heavier change,
   As when a rose is ruined by long rain
And the rich hues show rust; a sorrow strange
   Brooded within her eyes, and the wet stain
Tarnished her cheeks, as to mine own thought's range
   She sighed: "There is no love where I have lain!"

1916

SONGS TO FORGET I AM
A MORTAL

LOSSES

—Qu'as-tu fait, ô toi que voilà
Pleurant sans cesse.
Dis, qu'as-tu fait, toi que voilà,
De ta jeunesse?
—Verlaine

O you there weeping alone so bitterly,
What is it you weep for, paying bitterly
   The price in tears and darkened sunless eyes?
Only your youth?—yet always late or soon
Age scatters dust for gold and, late or soon,
   Darkens and then calms the desiring eyes.

But I am weeping my age which was so fair.
Nothing, not even death, was quite so fair.
   Mine was that wisdom in which the seraphs love,
And in my age agelessly I had been
Rose in the cherubs' rose-flame love—have been
   A golden mirror for the sun of love!

1916

IN THE WIND

Yellow clowns in an enormous pantomime,
The severed leaves rush over the green baize
In the sunlight,
Tumble, somersault, whirl,

208

Rush to the wings,
While in a flash of crimson
Some delirious columbine
Pirouettes, wheels, lifts in the air,
And sinks in a slow agony of delicious grace.

Do you not think, Elspeth,
Seeing how light it is,
Crisp and curling and forever dying,
That we should wear the scorn of death in our hearts,
Like a black relic pressed to a nun's white bosom?

CALM

It is deep afternoon, Elspeth, the wind has gone.
The poplar is a green water under the dawn
With a shiver of silver turning the smooth green.
The dead leaves are crumpled into gold on the green,
The dead leaves that are crushed into sound as we pass,
Like the swish of a long scythe through the summer grass.

The wise have held that only sorrow makes us wise;
So I think, and when I look into your gracious eyes,
That I must surely be the foolishest man alive.
Is it not brave, Elspeth, brave but to be alive?
The wind is back and changing the lights in your hair.
See how the maple shakes its red mane in the air.

THE SNOW

Elspeth, I can but guess the vague shape of the sky;
    It is all greyness and moving flecks on a glare.
God must be young, Elspeth, young and less wise than I
    To shred his sky so and scatter it on the air.

White buds are puffing into white bloom on the trees;
  The dark pines are petalled with a soft burst of snow;
The dark pines are dense with numberless white bees,
  Which swarm at the scentless bloom, hover, whirl and blow.

Soon we shall be as a light drift of snow—poor ghosts
  Threading some labyrinth of air. Then—ah! but now
My heart is the heart of a child, a child that boasts
  No then, but stops and laughs at the white-pelted bough.

IN SUCH A GARDEN . . .

Ah! Elspeth, that slow curve of the moon
Through the dense leaves—
How like the rounding of perfect fruit it is!
Of perfect fruit in ancient gardens
Where green and bronze and violet unfold
In the stately procession of peacocks.

In such a garden . . .

It seems to me that we have had no past,
No past with its old sorrows and dead joys;
And now there is to be no more gladness . .
But it may be I am foolish,
And . . .

Lean your head.
So the moonlight shifts to your shoulder,
And your hair is a pale and perilous wonder.
Ah! your lips now.

In such a garden . . .

There should be peacocks on the open grass
And a great basin to blur
Its shadows of dark green and pallors of silver.

IN THE BEGINNING

I had dreamed that Love would come under broad pennons of
    gold,
With rumbling of ponderous drums and conches braying,
Straying of crimson,
Bickering of banners blown to vermilion and gold,
With brown-burnt faces under barbaric turbans,
And a tumult of hoofs upon stony pavements.

And Love has come . .
But quietly as a girl who walks
With bare feet over the warm grass
In a night of moths and roses.

DEFEAT

I had thought to bring you all things,
And I bring
Only the banners of my defeat,
Banners that were bright as faith,
Terrible as life,
And full of tumultuous beauty like desire.

They hang dead now,
Dead and silent,
Their gold tarnished and their crimson rust.

See how they shake a little dust from out their folds!

MUSIC

When music was made I listened,
    For sounds were no longer sound,
But green and silver glistened
    Where leaves and dew were found.

And the sweet sounds trembling together
   Were flakes of unsounding snow,
Or faded leaves in a weather
   Of windy ebb and flow.

When music is made I never
   Shall see such things again;
For never shall I dissever
   Loveliness now from pain.
Your lips and your eyes will haunt me,
   As light is haunted by shade,
And the thing that has not been taunt me,
   Now when music is made.

THE BIRDS OF PARADISE

I have seen the Birds of Paradise
   Afloat in the heavy noon,
Their irised plumes, their trailing gold,
Their crested heads, like flames grown cold;
   They rose and vanished soon.

Strange dust is blown into mine eyes;
   I doubt I shall ever see
Their lightly lifted forms again,
   Their burning plumes of holy grain,
   And this is grief to me.

THE TRIUMPH OF DOUBT

There is so much loveliness gone out of the world!
   There is left but the violet dusk of the wood
      And the slow wavering of grey-blue hills on the sky.
The dead grass is silent and the dead leafage whirled
      Down the long lanes of silent air. The barberry
   Drips from its twisted crown of thorns slow drops of blood.

These are the days when the soul is less than a leaf
 Blown through the shrivelled grass or left on the frozen sod;
  For these, if they fail, fail with one more sure than they.
Now doubt stands long by the murdered bed of relief
 And feels for his own side; the soul stares at decay,
 Then turns slowly, triumphantly, swiftly to God.

ENDYMION IN A SHACK

I love the white body of the moon,
   And I think that she loves mine
For its strong limbs, brown and firm as sands
   Left with a watery shine.

There are no windows where I sleep,
   But a shaky, crooked stair
Climbs through the wind and the wind-swept trees,
   And the caked snow crunches there.

And there she climbs through the silent night
   And sweeps through the gusty door,
And the sudden light of her soundless feet
   Beats on the white-oak floor,

As she crosses and whispers into my ears
   Words more than wisdom wise,
And lays her slow blue bands of light
   Over my fearful eyes.

1917

SIGHTS

Eastern Virginia

As I went down to Millville,
   A hill on either han',

214

I saw two dirt-black nigger boys
　　Drivin' a load o' san'.

As I went into Millville
　　Along the gray stone road,
I only saw the miller's man
　　Storin' a farmer's load.

Oh! Millville's small an' dirty,
　　An' there one only fin's
Black windowpanes an' low black roofs
　　An' men with evil min's.

As I came out o' Millville
　　Along the red clay lane,
I saw a girl with pale gol' hair
　　Who looked at me again.

As I went up from Millville,
　　For good two hours' ride,
I saw the glint o' strange gray eyes
　　An' nothin' else beside.

1917

MUSHROOMS

Cold toadstools under moist moons growing
　　Push up between rain-rusted leaves
　　And rank wet growths which August eves
Vex, when dull winds blowing
　　Bring clouds of thin vibrating wings,
　　In damp dusk woods where morning clings
After the morning, and the gray even
Flits like a moth under no starlit heaven.

Dead-flesh-like where the quick flesh holds them,
  With a thick odor of rich mold,
  As when things oversweet grow old
And slow decay enfolds them;
  Above as a snake's summer skin
  Smooth, but below void veins begin
To vex the bloodless frozen flesh
With labyrinthine line and glutted mesh.

White with a cold unhealthy whiteness,
  Black with the blackness of bruised blood,
  Rose-purple, like a feverish bud
Filled with unhappy brightness,
  Where the sharp winds bite hard like flame;
  They rise as though some poisonous name
By demons spoken under earth
Had set them there with smiles of sterile mirth.

1916

LEAF-GREEN

(A *Ballad of the Blue Ridge*)

As I went up the Blue Ridge
  I came by Barton Stone,
And the night was a night of leaves and light
  Through leafless spaces blown.

I passed into the deep forest,
  And the dark night closed me round;
The dark spray flung its mist in my eyes,
  The boughs crashed, and I found

A level space of dew and grass
  Under a quiet moon,
And in the broken shade a dwarf
  Plucking a quiet tune.

Straight from his crooked back uprose
    The chestnut's shaggy bark,
And over his wizened pallor fell
    Stray fragments of the dark.

And where no leaves withheld the moon
    A lovely lady was,
Pacing a dance whose edges swept
    The edges of the grass.

With flowers her loosened hair was bound,
    And broken laurel buds;
Her sleeves were green as the leaves are green
    That stir in the inner woods.

"And who are you, sweet lady,
    That dance alone by night,
With shivering veils of silken green
    And hair like a shadowy light?

"Your sisters died in England—
    Three hundred years are gone—
And never a ship could cleave the seas
    'Twixt darkening east and dawn.

"Oh! who are you, sweet lady,
    Green-clad, with lightsome foot,
Who touch nor crush the white mushroom
    That grows at the chestnut root?"

But still she danced, and still she danced,
    And not a sound was there,
But the pressed grass and the plucked lute
    Making a plaintive air.

And still she danced, and her courtseys were
    As boughs that feel the rain;
Danced, and the fluttering silks were leaves
    When the light has come again,

Swept low with waving arms—and left
    The leaves and the moon-swept green
And a gnarled and twisted chestnut root
    Where the crooked dwarf had been.

CAMPBELL HALL

Night over Princeton is all drenched through with blue;
Over the blue slate and black massed shadows, blue;
And through it all, out of the thin light,
Weaving a golden web for golden flies,
The tragic spider of the skies,
The moon. Over Princeton, space and blue night.
It is there, it is there,
So keenly that it gives us pain!
We that are so young that it gives us pain
Feel still a cold wind moving through our hair.

You there under the eaves,
Your light
Ruffling with yellow the wet leaves,
You lover of Shelley, shut away from night,
Say, did you think
Because we did not wear
The bare white throat, the disordered hair,
The fine romantic dress,
The pale luxury of despair,
That space torments us less?
Oh! we are tired of waiting by a chink
Which never widens to light.

Now, it is a necromancer's robe of blue,
With gold worked through,
With pentagons of the color of gold and points of light.

1917

FEBRUARY 1917

Nothing moves me but mine own thoughts:
Not the fine hatred of war,
Nor the hatred which war brings forth.

But all my nights are filled with a violet-blue dusk
      of dreams,
And through the dusk
The ripple of silk over white flesh
And the wistful eyes of immortal women.

Nothing shakes my pulse but mine own dreams.

But all night long I see,
Ceaselessly falling,
Filled with light,
Distilling a rare fragrance,
Hair that is neither of silver nor gold,
Hair that is neither like silver nor gold,
But beaten of some unsearchable metal,
Softer than silver,
More lustrous than gold.

And yet, if the call should come,
I should go down with the rest,
And take my turn with the festered limbs of men,
The broken brains and the bruised eyes,
And the dead that have no more dreams.

NASSAU STREET

Oh! it's a brave show the small shops are making,
    Washed and made fair by suns and winds of spring;
The windows stir, and the gold light comes flaking
    Down from each sign with its shrewd lettering.

One, two, there are gray walls and pale-green shutters—
    Three, four—pink walls and shutters of dark green;
And over each the one flag lifts and flutters,
    Ripples its blue, folding the stars between,

And curls its crimson like flames about a martyr,
    Fills with the wind and trembles like a thought.
The villagers draw near, pass on, linger and barter,
    And haply see and haply see it not.

But we—we've given our all, our love of living,
    Youth, joy, and hope—for these were ours to give.
One thought they were, but one, past all forgiving:
    That these should be and freedom cease to live.

How should we save when freedom stood a claimant,
    Whose light was ours as freely as the sun?
What was to give but all, and for repayment,
    Less than the praising word for work well done?

Laurel—maybe some darker leaf than laurel
    Shall find our brows insensate as the clay—
It matters not. This is the supreme quarrel,
    And the end comes. What word is there to say?

Princeton, New Jersey,
    April 1917

TO TOWNSEND MARTIN

I had many things to bring you, ambergris and cinnamon,
    Couched in ebon coffers or in ivory divine:
    Rounded fruits and grapes in clusters, grapes to make you
      wine,
Colored like the midnight and tasting of the sun.

Here I come, and here my gifts are. I lay them at your feet.
    Spotted fruit and bitter fox-grapes, plundered by the rain.
    They are all my garden proffers, and I shall not go again
To the spring-delighted gardens where our ways were wont to
      meet.

I had many things to give you—cinnabar and cassia,
    And such fruits as round and ripen in the sunnier air.
    I had many songs to sing you—but I know not what they were;
Here my gifts are—take or leave them—for I go another way.

From THE UNDERTAKER'S GARLAND
1922

From THE UNDERTAKER'S GARLAND

LUCIFER *

I plodded homeward through the snow and stubble,
  A wallet heavy with junk upon my back,
And saw the sun, a fire-distended bubble,
  Sway over the stiff trees grown flat and black.
And as the sun, perceptibly descended,
  Tumbled a cloud of carmine to the snow,
A god came striding through the tree boles, splendid
  In pride of youth, naked, bearing a bow.
I dropped my pack and raced across the hollow,
  Stumbled, and sank knee-deep in drifts, and cried:
"God of the silver bow, divine Apollo,
  It is not true that you with Hellas died!"
    With the profound tenderness of a sage or brother,
  The god turned, and tremendous thunder flamed:
"Apollo died long ago. I am that other
  Who sang. For me the morning star was named."

Cir. 1920

* This poem appeared as the Prologue to *The Undertaker's Garland* (1922),
a volume of poetry and fiction by Bishop and Edmund Wilson.—*Editor.*

THE DEATH OF A DANDY

Le Dandy doit aspirer à être sublime,
sans interruption. Il doit vivre et
dormir devant un miroir.
      —Charles Baudelaire

The exquisite banality of rose and ivory:
Shadows of ivory carved into panels, stained
And decayed in the moulding; rose-colour looped
Casting a shadow of mauve; blown cherubs
Bulging in silver,
Lift six tapers to the lighted mirror.

A dusk, deep as the under side of a rose,
Is curtained under the old bed-dome.
Contracting the coverlet, a shape lies
Which may or may not be a man.

What thoughts should an old man have
In the London autumn
Between dusk and darkness?
Behind the shrunken eyelids, what apparitions?
What pebbles rattle in a dry stream?

A boy with a pale, lovely, dissolute face
Sprawled on the green baize, among the cards,

A Spanish pistol dropped from one hand—
Seen from the glazed squares of the club, a street
Cobbled with faces, bundles of rags and lice,
A yellow dwarf rising with protruding face—
Gilded Indian gamecocks clawing blood
Amid the clapping of pale hairless hands—
Lady Barfinger, masked in satin, disclosing her gums,
Labored graces of a cracked coquette—
A Jew that came on sliding haunches,
Crouched, and with distended palms
Whined for his pledges—Alvanley,
Embroidered in silver foil, poised at the court,
The ball a mirror of silvery Alvanleys.

Phantoms under a cloudy ceiling, uneasy images,
Sentences that never come to a period.
Thoughts of an old dandy shrunk to a nightgown.

The chamfered fall of silken rose—
Muffling London and the autumn rain—
Lifts and recurves,
A beautiful young man,
Naked, but for a superb white tiewig,
Moves in with slow pacings of a cardinal
Dreaming on his cane.

The firelight blushes on the suave
Thighs of the young man, as he glides
From his calm, with an inessential gesture
To brush his tiewig. Palm upon knuckles,
Fingers over the cane head, he regards
Amusedly his own face in the crystal.
"Without my powdered curled peruke
I were but a man; so, I am a dandy.

For what was there to do, being no god
Burnished and strong, amorous of immortals,
But to escape this disappointing body
Punily erect, patched with scant hair,
Rank in its smell too,
By hiding it in silk and civet—adding to silver hair,
Pomp of vermilion heels?
What else, indeed, unless to drown
All naked, to drown all sense in wine.

"They thought my wit was all in waistcoats,
My epigrams pointed but with dainty tassels,
When every ribbon that my fingers tied
Protested with a fragile indolent disdain
A world exquisitely old and dull and vain.
So I gave them my jest—
Walking stark naked to the gaming room
Where the preened dandies leaned across their cards,
Their pale long fingers spread among the cards.

"They laughed: I did not laugh: so old
So pitiful, so brutal and so dark
The buffoonery. But the body's the jest of Another—
I make my obeisance."

Young Coatsworth has become
A naked glimmer on the lighted glass,
Fainter than the shimmer among rainy bees.

An old man lies propped on a bed.
Counting the candles of the empty glass—
An old man who has seen
His own youth walking in the room.

The window silk puffs with a winter gust,
And Coatsworth, *aetatis suae* XXV,
Flapped in gold braid crinkled in air-blue,
With inscrutable precision
Bows in a lady,
Who repeats the scene with the graces of a marionette.

"Madam," he says, addressing her panniers,
"Your bodice is miraculously a double moonrise,
Your throat the traditional swan's white—
But fuller. Your lips an exciting cochineal.
But in truth, love is at best
A fashionable intrigue, an accompliced secret,
Unendurable without grated orris root.
Love remains to the proud mind
A ladder loosened from the brazen tower,
A furtive flight from the sentineled domain
Where self is utterly contained in self.
Though you ordered the death of a thousand roses,
I've caught the breath of a garden, where
No man has ever been, and the ripe fruit
Drops through the tarnished air
Unheeded, and yew trees are made peacocks.
I thank you for your horrible favours.
Adieu—"

The lady unravels to a ragged smoke:
Coatsworth darkens with blood like a satyr,
Blushes in a burnish on the mirror,
Burns and is gone.

The dry skull stretches regretful claws
And the points of the tapers twist and bend—
Sallow fingers of Jewish usurers.

A rapier flicks through the curtains
Like a needle of sunlight splintered on the sea.
Coatsworth presses before him,
Back to the fireplace, a panting stripling.
A jet of wet red spurts from the shirt front;
The youth sinks and dribbles in blood through the carpet.

"The end of such upstart heralds
As would bar my shield to the sinister."
The reflected visage is rigid,
Puckered thinly with wrinkles.
"What if I got my finger's trick,
Whether with rapiers or a puffing neck-cloth,
From a confectioner of Bath
Whose fastidious years were spent
Tracing on cakes sweet labyrinths of ice,
Squeezing pink fondant into petalled buds?
What that, overnight, through an open window,
He got me because a crooked pear tree
Climbed to the window ledge?
No man's to call me bastard.
And what's a murder more or less
Amid the inane fecundity of blood and sweat.
A barmaid and a groom repair the loss."

The dead youth has subsided in blood
Leaving the floor unsoiled.
Coatsworth has leapt through the silvered glass
Leaving its flames unspoiled.

His pallor stained by the rose-dimmed dusk,
An old man lies on a curtained bed,
Whimpering like a beggar in a wet loft
When the wind's found the cracks and the straw is cold.

Coatsworth, now old, steps from the window folds
With a gesture consciously tragic;
Stands for a moment
Half Don Juan, half Childe Harold;
Then stalks, a magpie motley
Black, buff and silver, up to the mirror.
He regards the vain, brave fall
Of the surtout, the triple tied neck-cloth,
The bronze hair brushed as in busts of Nero—
Then with a posture almost Byronic
Confides in silence.

"Amid the bumpers, the scaffoldings, the ilex cones,
I have ever worn the scorn of death
With the careless grace of a boutonnière.
But let me be buried with a fiery choir;
A scarlet and lace processional of boys,
And priests too old to lift their stiffened folds
Too wise to hold their clouded incense as a prayer.
Tie up my chin lest I should smile.
And press into my hand my laurel cane
Where Daphne with blown crinkled hair
Feels the hard wood invade her silver thighs;
Leave me my snuff box for its musty yawn
And for its intricate cool ivory
Showing an April faun at his desires;
Probate my will, offer my house for rent.

"I had thought to find a languor, to attain
A gallant erudition in the snuff box and the cane;
To restore a tarnished splendour
Ceremonious as a stole,
Gorgeous like a vestment—yet urbane;
Between the opening and the closing of the doors

To have stood between the sconces, ripe in silk,
Ancestral laces falling to the sword;
Reflected in the parquetry, to dream
Of Giorgione in a tricorn, and high wigs
Powdered with palest silver, piled like clouds;
Of odorous mummied roses, grown dusty with a queen
Tender and slight and proud.

"But I have stood so long
Before so many mirrors, I'm afraid,
Afraid at last that I may be
A shadow of masks and rapiers between the girandoles
A satin phantom, gone when the wax is down."

He becomes a toothless grimace
Between the moveless cherubs, silver blown.

Under the lustered bed-dome, in the curtained dusk,
A throat moans—the sudden and lonely
Cry of one ridden by a nightmare,
Who wakes and finds it is no dream.

Old Coatsworth unravels from the bed clothes—
As ghost unwinding its buried linen,
And stands, toes clutched and indrawn,
Ridiculously muffled in linen ruffles;
Totters slowly to the glass
To find therein, grinning wide with terror,
The toothless mist of the last apparition.
Shrieking, he plucks a candle from its socket
And drives the double flame into the darkness.
Another, another, another,
Four tapers extinguish their windy stains
In a smear of wax on the mirror.

Another flame drops from a bony claw.
Like the drums of a defeat, a heart sounds.
And he peers at the dwindling face in the mirror—
The face of a dandy brought to a shroud.

Clutching the last tremulous candle
The old dandy sways,
Clings to the air,
And sinks in a slow movement of exhausted mirth.

The mirror is heavy with shadows
And a white candle spreads a film on the hearthstone.

THE FUNERAL OF AN UNDERTAKER

I

Shrunken by life to a hard grin,
Alone upon an unkempt bed,
The man whose labouring years had been
A watch with death himself lay dead.

His eyes stared at the ceiling; the chin
Had fallen; one sleeveless arm was thrown
Limply across the bed, the skin
Pulled thin to fit each finger bone.

Though all men knew that he was dead
No waxlight burned beside his bed.

And no one from the village came
With black boards for a coffin frame.

No housewife came to bind his mouth
With a smooth strip of linen cloth.

No prayer was said, and no one swung
The bell rope where the church bell hung.

II

Year after year the villagers had watched
The gutters lose their evening stains,
The skies descend and the grey dusk
Hang cobwebs on the windowpanes,
And by a yellowing street lamp seen
A hurrying coat of blistered green
Clutched by one hand, meagre and blotched
With colourless spots like a bad husk,
A shabby hat crushed low as if
To mask the eye they had not seen—
And pressed upon the sill and said:
"So the old buzzard's got a whiff,
He'll soon be pecking at the dead."
And some of them there were that leaned
Hard on the windowpanes and turned
Sallow as though he were the fiend
And they were souls which he had earned.
None knew how long since he began—
How many nights since first he held
A dripping candle to lidless eyes
And peering let the hot wax fall
On lips composed for burial.
None knew how long since he began
To probe the dust heaps of the spirit
And finger dusty histories;
But slowly this washer of the dead discerned
What droll, half-earnest clowns inherit
The mask and tragic rôle of man.
Not even the child who heard his tread
Scuffling the autumn leaves and rain

Could guess what unpersuadable pities
Drove him forth to walk the rain,
Or how this lonely washer of the dead
Was by his own deep passion comforted,
Until he had grown old as ancient cities
That have looked so many times upon their slain.

Keeping no thought of slackened blood,
Less vigorous bone or tardy mind,
He watched a vain and dwarfish brood
Chatter at tasks which chance assigned,
Seeking in toil what poets scarcely find
Among the shadows of the immortal wood.
And always at the one moment when
His despised craft had power on men
He sought with patient pitiless care,
With visible wit, to make aware
What puffed, unprofitable things had borne
His bitter and compassionate scorn.

With starved horse and bare hearse he gave
The poor in spirit to the grave;
And nailed the comfortably good
In coffins of worm-eaten wood;
He showed the niggardly and mean
By hiding under ropes of green,
Small gaudy flowers and bits of vine
Their yellow coffins of cheap pine.
With hearse and hack on polished hack,
Tacky with trappings of crimped black,
He set the opulent and loud
Before the dumb, lip-fallen crowd.
But those who'd looked in bewilderment on
The unintelligible sun,
Who might have leapt with a cry and bled

Their youth out on a barricade;
All those whose frustrate hearts had cried
For braver beauty, and so died,
Crumpled and dry, broken like a clod
Too many heels have trod—
To these a slow processional
Was given—a silver drooping pall,
Falling in sheeny folds which shifted
Stiffly as violent horses lifted
Black crests of thick plumes and drew
The dim pomp to the grave.

                    But few
He found among his kith and neighbours
Who earned such honour of his labours:
Some nine there were and of these five
He'd known but slightly when alive.

So he had lived, tormented, proud
As a poet, hated by the crowd
That paunched and bred and plied a trade,
Kept small accounts and sometimes prayed
To an old god with untrimmed beard
Who kept accounts and slily peered
Into the things too slily done;
Who made the moon and trimmed the sun.
And all these when they heard him dead,
Shrugged their bones and sniffed and said,
"Good riddance to the village, then;
He was a pest to honest men."

So now he lay, a poor, untended
Wrack of shrunk skin and jointless bone,
The man whose endless task was ended,
Whose anguish stifled like a groan.

All day a small insistent clock
Ticked and slid to the hours' mark
And rattling to a rusty shock
Hour by hour brought on the dark.

And with the dark a rat came out
And snuffed among stale bacon rinds
And chunks of bread; a leaking spout
Trickled; a gust flopped in the blinds.

And in the dark the dead man sprawled
Like one who'd stretched a bloody reign
And in his violent hour had called
Upon the household guards in vain.

III

The night is thin. The air is crisp,
For the spring is scarcely felt at night.
The air is still with a windy lisp
Where the first leaves in the thicket are.
The moon is misty as a star,
But the rounded stones are washed with white
And a chance spade glints with steely light.

There is no sound at the graveyard's edge
Save for the rustling hornbeam hedge;
But something shivers beneath the soil
As when a mole is at his toil;
Something struggles under the ground,
Thrusts the earth to a gritty mound,
Squirms and flutters, and suddenly there
Is a frail wisp upon the air,
Like the blue smoke of sodden leaves
Which children burn on autumn eves;

It writhes and gathers, shifts and breaks,
Thickens with colour, waves and takes
The semblance of a man long buried,
Old before death, his gaunt cheeks serried
With furrows where the rain has lain.
Another mound of grave-loam stirred;
A second gathered shape; a third,
Then five dead men, and one dead woman,
Cracking the ground at an unheard summon,
Out of the shapeless air unravel.
They glide without feet along the gravel
Between black borders of clipped box,
Brush through the wicket's spikes and locks,
Glide to the church, where no one tolls
Except for pay for dead men's souls;
Past the church and through the streets
Where smug wives snore between clean sheets
With every window shut and barred
And a restless watchdog in the yard.
Then at a word no lip had uttered
Into the dead man's house they fluttered
And there for a waiting moment stood
Like panting things of bone and blood,
And stared at the blind shape which there
Cluttered the green distorted square
The late moon in the window made.

For these of all whom he had laid
In the obscure and level earth,
These only he had thought of worth.
These alone had sought to enmesh
Ecstasy in the unholding flesh,
Or with stretched throats had stood
While drums and scarlet in the blood
Arrayed a triumph for the mind,

When raggedness or cold assigned
Their aching arms to swinging slops
To pigs or storing a farmer's crops;
And waking to the white rain
Pecking at the shingle roof had lain
Alone and awake, while with young breath
Through love of life they cried for death.
And these now from the grave were come,
In dumb and yearning shapes were come
To bear the dead man to his grave.
Four abrupt white tapers wave
At the four corners of the bed.
A sudden spectral gesture moulds
The hands to quiet, the feet to stone;
And circling shadows compose the dead
On a low bier of forgotten boards;
The moonlight through the bleared panes sifted
Falls on a pall of rigid folds
And tassels threaded with tarnished cords.
Then with a light of tapers lifted,
Shuffling as if to a monotone,
Out of the room, the narrow door—
Nodding beneath the lintel's beam—
The dumb, black-leaning phantoms bore
Their burden; and, as if seen through a stream,
Went wavering over the pavement stones,
Rocking as if their shoulders shook
Under the confused weight of bones.
No shutter's chink widened to look
With a quickened eye where in the drowned
Colour and glimmer of thin moonshine
The corpse-bearers shuddered without sound.
No window gaped for the watchdog's whine
As with its load the processional
Flickered by silent door and wall,

House by house, to the street's verge,
Where from a shadow against a light
It dwindled to shadow and merged
Into the phantasmal night.

THE DEATH OF GOD

My spirit is a bow unstrung,
My strength is as a twisted pod,
Yet I remember, once, a young
Exultant, wind-flushed, passionate god—
Who fled down the green colourless wave,
Burning the silence with a glittering scale,
Yet found no coral and no sea's floor;
Who plunged and soared and poised, but gave
Care to no thought but that his flail
Threshed a gold sheaf on an idle floor;
Who knew not whence he came, nor cared
While there remained that opening door
And a cloudy flight of palaces, staired
With mirrors, fragments of a separate sun.
Ages were woven and woven, unspun,
Before the delight of winnowed hair,
Of diving sheer from the whirlwind's brim,
Of feeling the runnels of space on bare
Unwearied limbs could weary him.
But slowly a questionless vast despair
Hooded his brain; on his heart an ache
Knocked like a sword against the thigh.
The winds were no longer stiff to slake
The thirst I had—for the god was I!
Centuries circled past with a cry
Like baying hounds. At last I arose
And plunged into the burning gyres
Where the intensest sun-slag glows,

And churned the spindrift till it whirled
Rocketing colours, metallic fires,
Vermilion, cobalt, frost and black-rose.
Urged by a blind, dark, sultry lust
I trampled the blazoned clouds of dust
Like a wild stallion in a pound—
Fire upon dust, dust upon spark—
Till a huge uncouth, unthought-of world
Went toppling blindly down the dark
With a hot unwieldy sound:
And wonder was there like a sudden wound!

Ages and ages were smuggled away
While I shaped with slowly subtle hand
A universe I had not planned:
Suns of inviolate sapphire burning
With stars to circle upon their light,
Choruses to one high voice returning;
Suns of amber and bluish light,
Shaken like dew on the boughs of night;
Comets with fluttering fetlocks and long tossing manes,
Plunging in triumph against their stiff reins,
Thudding a dust of white fire from their hoofs;
And the stars that have stars for company
When they sit at feast under heaven's roofs
And utter a sweet articulate cry.
Then out of a white wind wandering came
Lovely spirits nimbed in flame
Even against that illumined air;
Stripling they moved,
Bending each on each a remote stare
From arrogant eyes that were wise in love,
Dripping a sun's rain from smooth thighs
As they moved.
And some of them had strength enough

To have followed with speed, unsandalled, unmewed,
The galloping thunders of the sun;
And some wore pointed wings upon
Poised and tremulous heels, subdued—
With a thin crescent of lifted wings,
Ivory-rich misted with silver—the flame
Which dawned a rose ardour from bright hair
Kindled and unbound by the great pair
Which from their shoulders beat or fluttered.
But all were courteous in their pride
Save one, lucescent as his name,
Who, when he would have spoken, uttered
A thin cry, dropped to his knees, and gazed
Down where the stars were, intricately mazed
As gleams of green phosphorus in the tide;
Crouched in a glare like one who has sent
Thick bloodhounds on his own son's scent
And looks into a network of winds.
Then gathering to his feet
He made as if his hands would beat
A dancing measure; and a song
Demon-sweet and wild and strong
Made his face strange—a song of light
And colours wheeling in the light,
Vermilion, saffron, blue-green and blue,
And the blind and unimaginable hue
Which trembles beyond the terror of white;
All things that were and things unknown:
Blindness of suns and staggering stars,
The red-brass pomp of battle cars,
The scraping of spears against a throne.
And all that high unsorrowing throng
Were hid from each other by their tears,
And pressed white brows, because of the song
Which Lucifer made among his peers.

And I too, sitting among them there,
Knew beauty's intimate despair,
And dreamed of a green wide-islanded star
With one white moon to follow her,
A place where immortal beauty should sit
With mortal eyes to ponder it.

And afterwards I remember, remember,
We sat like stars in the sun's feast chamber,
And I shared with them my mind;
And brooding upon their litheness assigned
Each a rollicking planet to ride,
A moon to tame, or to sit upon
A huge, unruly, turbulent sun.
I taught them all my wit had learned,
How starry speed was qualified
By bulk and distance; why this one burned
And that rolled darkling: all that I knew
And all I guessed might well be true.
They leapt and clashed their ivory spears,
And shouted; and down through the regions of
            night and morn
Fled like partridges frightened from corn.
I turned that none might see my tears.

And after, long after, I shaped a star
With one white moon to follow her.
A place where immortal beauty should sit
With mortal eyes to ponder it.
There out of odour, sound and colour
I made those shapes which seemed to wear
In the bronze lustre of that undimmed air
A beauty elaborate and austere,
Which now is shadowed, or grown duller
Than an old man's wit to a young man's ear.

I made all forms of greenery
Under the air or beneath the sea:
The tree that like a fountain soars,
The tree that like a cloud downpours
In a rustling rain of silver leaves;
The tree whose petals are gold at noon
And moonlight coloured in the moon;
And every sort of tree that weaves
A net of leaves from limb to limb.
I made green beetles smouldering dim
And pheasants fanned to a golden glare
In the white furnace of the air:
And the many strange sea-breathing things
Which sprawl in jellies and coil in rings,
Dripping slow slime from viscous eyes
Amid the deep sea's forestries.
I made the spider obese and hairy
And taught him to spin and thread an airy
Web of colourless polygons,
And shook against the twisted skein
Cool bubbles of translucent dew,
Violet-gold, and irised rain
The first windy light comes through
When hills are lowered before the dawn.
And still I might feel my breath indrawn
Could I but see that murderous seine
Dredging fat flies from the streams of air
And ugliness dragging up unaware
The careless iridescent dawn.

I made when I had learned to smile
The knobbed and scaly crocodile,
Blue-buttocked, feathery-whiskered apes,
And monkeys with brown tendril shapes;
I made when I had learned to laugh

244

The painted ludicrous giraffe,
The sluggish hippopotamus,
Leathery, lewd, preposterous:
The dwarfed and bulked grotesquery
Under the winds and beneath the sea.

But beauty alone had terror
To lay delight on my youth, so that I shook
As when the first of morning ripples to clearer
Green the swift lustres of a brook,
And a naked bather wades and is chill.
Yet never was I so seamed with pain,
And for her sake, that not one vein
Was quiet, and carved in wind I ran,
As when the hour was come to fulfil
The breathing body of man.
Lying unstirred, one knee upturned,
Through ruddy loose hair and the broad
Sloped shoulders, down to the noble thigh, there burned
The gracious indolent ardour and
Cloudy repose of a god.
I breathed on his face, and my breath
Went sharp through his side; stretched out my hand—
A shudder of light tumbled his hair,
And he turned his sleep to a stare, aware
Of beauty and aware of death.
And something came back to my blood, I recalled
Lucifer's face, and the circled crowd—
Dim crescents of wings, flushed faces enthralled,
And the lifted throat despair had made proud!
It is long since I have done aught but look
Through blinkered eyes at images
Which once had halted my heart's blood,
As an old man shrunk to a hood
Sits quiet, pondering a book,

245

For which in his youth he had foregone ease,
Or the mouth of a girl, or gold.
Crouched over my bones and old,
I have long leaned chin upon wrist
And let my thought twist and untwist
Like a black weed dragged in a stream,
And wondered indeed if I exist,
Or am but the end of a dream.
Ah, why must all things come upon trouble
And all that sultry passion seem
A rustle of wind in the dry stubble—
Unless from the first I failed in thought?

The wheels of the chariots were wrought
Of purest bronze, but with a broken rim;
The unshod chargers fell in the long wars.
For all their silver ribaldry the stars
Go mad in their courses, a dry skull
Rots where the moon was beautiful;
The suns were pocked at birth with scars.

Oh, violent and young, distraught
And exulted with undrunk wine, I brought
Vast splendours from the earlier night,
Yet failed because I held in despite
The labour and repose of thought.
Is this shrunk star the flaming dream
Which came with islands and bright-scaled water,
Wheeling a dark and a radiant rim
As near and away from the sun it sped?
Was it for this I sought or
Sat in labour? for this that Lucifer
Sang, the unshadowable light-bearer?
And of man, of man, what shall be said?
I would my heart were piteous

That I might pity him! He lifts his head
So bravely to the sun, is amorous
Of beauty, conquest and delight;
Spends blood upon banners; drums the earth
With adventurous tramplings; shrills the air
With the insolent envy of his mirth.
What have I made of him? What—to requite
A love more desperate than despair?
A poor creature smeared with his own dung,
Who struts a little, being young,
And has scarcely sounded his own distress
Before he has crumbled to rottenness.
Distinguished on a gilded couch
He mutters under his dying breath
Of some old plan of lust or wrath,
Unaccomplished, beyond his touch.
Or left beneath a broken rafter
Crouched on a straw heap, unwarmed, alone,
A stench of frayed flesh about a bone,
He counts that best which never was,
Remembering how the wise drew laughter,
And dead madmen were accounted wise;
How lovers had but their blinded eyes
And Caesar's armies a tune of brass.

Has the sun no molten core where I may be hid?
Is there no penitential fire to shrive me?
O man, man, man, forgive me,
I wrought, not knowing what I did!
I will start up, dragging these bones
Knee after knee,—if it must be,
Drag this loose strength, knee after knee,
And come at last on the shaken thrones
Of the last golden dynasties
Of time; startle the suns, and leave their skies

A smouldering heap of palace stones
Set in the flaring dusk of a city
Where none is loud for pain or for pity.
I will loose the stars from their high stud
And lash their heavy-hooved stampede
Till foundering they darken, broken with speed;
Dabble the moon's face with earth's blood,
That not one man shall be left at length
To taunt me with enduring youth.

I have forgot—I have no strength!
I am gnawn clean by a ravening tooth.
The blood in my wrist is so sucked and thinned
I cannot drag my beard from the wind
Where its ravelled cords are tossed and lying.
It is not man but god who is dying!
But how had I known that a god should grow old
And his bright hair thin to a streaked whiteness,
His beard fall long and clotted with mould
Whose heart had been as the dawn for lightness?
How had I dreamt that at last I should look
On the stars in their tumult, and find such pain
In a world I had thought to have made without stain
That my head would sink in my elbow's crook,
My throat give sobs in the place of breath,
My mouth ask easily after death?

My face is turned toward death, and yet,
Weak, bewildered and blind, I grope
Still for the unappeasable hope
That sleep, not death, shall touch my brain,
And touch my eyelids, and restore
Youth and all youth lacked before.
It may be I shall start up again
And put on strength like golden greaves

To the oily shins of a young man set,
And shake the stars till they fall like leaves
In an autumn drift along the air;
Know tumult again and wisdom, and tear
In the delighted lust of my heart
The broad beams of the world apart,
To build again, in another kind,
The orbs and whirlwinds of my mind.

THE MADMAN'S FUNERAL

"Pape Satan, pape Satan aleppe!"

The wind was bitter as a curse
Above the little pavement where
The mourners waited with the hearse
To bear the madman to his crypt;
There was no colour in the air;
The very trees stood lank and stripped.

Somewhere behind the listening doors
The living lifted up the dead.
We heard the creaking of the floors;
We heard their slow unheeding tread;
Dimly we saw six shadows—then
Six shadows stiffened into men.

And all at once there rose a squeal
And a startled devil leapt and slid
Along the madman's coffin lid,
A runty devil white and plump
As mushrooms by a rotten stump;
His eyes were sharp as pins of steel.

And swooping after swift as flame
And dark as blood that's partly dried,
On tilted feet a second came;
Who sliding from the coffin rim
Hopped to the hearse and climbed inside,
Pulling the other after him.

And there behind the polished glass
They grinned like monkeys in a cage.
Four demons paced with studied pomp
Down the slow steps, rump bruising rump,
Moaning as if in feeble rage.
And last one visaged like an ass

Flicked his hoofs to a two-heeled trot,
Scraping a rusty violin,
Held between nose and hairy hand;
He tripped behind the impious band
And to the tune of an old gavotte
Wheezed a low catch called "Love's a Sin."

The crowd gave way; the living bore
The dead man to the hearse's floor.
The demons gaped like routed whores,
Baying a dirge profane and loud;
While those within sat on the corse
And thumbed their noses at the crowd.

Then with a shout they broke and ran
To find them each a cushioned seat;
One goatish, hairy and unclean
Beside the clergyman was seen.
And whispering to that holy man
Rode smirking through the village street.

The one whose shape was like an ass
Moved sidling to the hearse's wheel,
And seeing where the coachman was,
And a bare space beside him there,
Leapt through the intervening air
With a click of heel on horny heel.

Amid the hearse's decent plumes
Strange music sagged from strings and bone;
And one whose eyes were fierce with pride
Sought out the place I kept alone.
I smelt the smell of opened tombs
When he had climbed inside.

Silk violet gloves episcopal
Made suave the talons of his claws;
His paunch let yellow foldings fall
Upon the shrunken thighs; he smiled,
Clasping a gesture of applause.
A whip cracked out; drab hackneys filed.

I saw the people left and right
Stare fearfully before a sight
So solemn, fat and atheous.
"Alas for us!" the demon said,
"God is a dolt to use us thus;
Where shall we rest now *he* is dead?

"But, oh! what sport we had of him!
Not since the great King Solomon
Lost his ring at the world's rim
And all the demons under sea
Stretched their wings and sought the sun
Has any known such jollity."

Through ends of streets the cortège wound:
On either side the houses stood,
Huddled, uncared for, skulls of wood,
Black windows socketed with eyes.
The demon's throat grew thick with sound:
"The madman once was otherwise.

"Joy was his in the clear light
And in the colours of the air,
In rooms where skilful violins
Renewed his adolescent sins;
Love was his, and in his sight
One fair woman seemed more fair.

"We crept on him with swaying tread;
Through sleeves and fingers whispering,
Shaped words so lewd and blasphemous
That love became a leprous thing.
We laughed each night beside his bed
Till God's own laughter answered us.

"And still we whispered, 'Love is lust,
The blue but grey, a broken tune
Outtops the mouth of melody.'
We turned the earth to stinking dust,
We dimmed the sun and left the moon
A twisted penny in the sky.

"We sucked his pores with pallid lips,
We mirked the blood within his heart,
We drove him forth with iron whips,
We scourged him back with bloody rods;
Then drew him to a place apart
To intimate this work was God's."

The carriages began to wind
Into a place of mounds and stones,
Hedges of bronze-green box and yews
Green-black and clipped to curious cones.
The fiend resumed: "Tonight I choose
Another nicely fashioned mind."

The carriage stopped. The corpse went by
And shadows in stiff folds of black.
I looked into the demon's eye
And saw therein, circled with fire,
My own eyes staring. I left the hack,
And with the fiend plashed through the mire.

We reached the grave. I looked and peered,
Nor saw a devil anywhere;
But straight the coachman seized a fife
And played an old and ribald air;
And through the prayers the parson leered
With hot eyes at the sexton's wife.

Behind the fir tree of his aunt's
Ungainly tomb, the grocer found
A fiery flask; a crape veil shrieked
And passed into a rigid trance;
And a boy laughed. The grave ropes creaked,
The coffin sank into the ground.

Earth, falling stone and gritty clay
Resounded from the coffin lid;
Spades crunched on earth and scraped on stone;
Earth fell; at last a low mound hid
The place where the madman's body lay.
The crowd dispersed. I stood alone.

I dared not move. A sudden dread
Was on me lest I turn my head
And see naught but the frozen sod
And the stiff trees which twilight blurred;
For in my thought I shaped a word
Cruel and meaningless as God.

UNCOLLECTED EARLY POEMS
1917-1923

UNCOLLECTED EARLY POEMS

IN A CAB

Quick flicking of horses' hoofs over cobbles
  And the soft burr of droning wheels.

Why is it with us Love always wears
The faded green coat of an old coachman?

No matter—for shining green broadcloth
Is a convenient screen for our love-making.

Drive slowly, good coachman,
For the afternoon is all dust and gold,
And I would have a long look at the houses.

1920

YOUTH AND DEATH

(For a drawing by Sydney Joseph)

Youth, pausing at the outer portal,
Felt the music surge as a dawn in the blood;
Saw through the open doors the immortal
White loveliness of dancers flash and move
In trembling ecstasy to the music's mood
And, suddenly lonely in the terror of love,
Stood hesitant and dumb. Then to her side
Came Death, hooded in thick black, pale and hollow-eyed,
Who, seeing how in Youth's eyes the moment burned,

Rose-flame, a clear and windless radiance,
Cried: "Remember all the beauty that is turned
Wearily to the dust; loves toward which no lovers call;
And feet that stir not now for any dance."
And Youth—that was and is love's thrill—
Replied: "Love draws its richness from the dust;
And beauty, passing in its April bloom,
Had not that perilous device we know,
But for some queen who, long ago,
Covered her golden hair with rust
Where some old town crashed to a crimson doom."

1920

FRANKIE AND JOHNNIE

*(As John Peale Bishop thinks it might be done by Ezra Pound
in his later and more disconnected manner)*

Damn it all, I have not forgot America—
Ricordate di me; sono lo pio [1]—
There was a song I heard in a smoker,
Not found in a bookstall—the book with broken hinges—
Not Arnaut now, nor Cavalcanti.

At Neuvic, in the blue Dordogne,
A grotto, grey-green, the lighting by Da Vinci,
Whither the old countess was moved from her bedchamber
To ripple the silvery pool, bathing her ankle,
Lancan son passat li giure—
Mine's the trick of a false beginning!

A *lupinaria* slit with two posterns
In some nether quarter, Chicago or the Lehigh Valley—
There's my setting, now for the phantastikon.

---

[1] I don't know that this pun is justifiable, *pio* having lost the primary meaning
of *pius*, but it may serve to annoy the Dante scholars and the academicians.
                                                                    —J. P. B.

Stalking with delicate tread amid the sparrows,
Venus's sparrows, a house-drab, stabbed with jealousy,
Seeks with a gun and a Winelout's connivance
After her lover. "He was my man,
But he done me wrong"—so the stave hath't.
Lugete, Veneres!

Charles Baudelaire, hair green like a drowned man's,
Sang in sonnet, loved in his life rather,
A negress, *bizarre, sorcière au flanc d'ébène:*
So this Johnnie—who it seems was rich in kisses,
Basiationnes (I improvise on the cadence)
Which through the solid sunlight, lustful, with golden
Greaves and breastplates [2] drew, or might have drawn
To his fall an archangel.
I crack my wit and close the canzone.

1921

SONNETS

From Porphyrio the Mad Prince to the Princesse Lointaine

I

Your hair is rufulous as the puffed rust
Blebbing a musket stock, vermicular
As the crimped locks stringing from the coif are
In Niccolò Fiorentino's bust
Of D'Este. Your odor carries no disgust
So long as rose-verbena haunts your silk cymar
And glaives of heat are not allowed to scar
Your skin that's thin as fish-scales. Yet unbussed
Your mouth pouts like a lethal red mushroom
Blistering spongy tree trunks in a wood
Anfractuous with boles and stumps. Assume

---

[2] *Vide autem* Lustra: *Three Cantos.*

I am a wooden horse hauled or stood
To please some small Ulysses in the blood,
Is it not clever, this, your toppling doom?

II

O dearest planet, suffer an eclipse
Of silence! Much too long your speech has shone!
Your body is a fountain of white stone
Green blistered by the trickling mouth which drips
A viridescent glaze over the hips'
Rondure and down to the knees. A knuckle bone
Drubbed on a drunken table has a tone
Less cacotechnical than your two lips.
Regarding you acutely one divines
God's fatal penchant for the incomplete;
Yet I suppose not to uphold your hair
Against my brains were an adventure meet
Only for lank ephebes and androgynes—
But here I spunge a thought from Baudelaire.

PORTRAIT FOR A BACKGROUND OF FLAT GOLD

It may well have been that my thought was heady
Or that lone drinking had spoiled my blood,
But I saw a cloud-staring lady
Ride into the light that edged a wood.

By the slim pressure of white knees
She swayed the pride of a unicorn
To swerve between the sapling trees
And score the leaves with his silver horn.

Picked up by the wind, her hair was lost
In a flutter of light against the sun;
Riding she caught in a scarf or tossed
Above her a smooth black-polished stone.

260

Suddenly she stopped and gazed
As though her eyelids twitched with soot;
Spurred with her heels; galloped and grazed
My trembling hand with her warm foot.

'Where has he gone'— she leaned her head—
'Who had so sweet a weight of limb,
Whose hair was red as the lion's is red?
It is long since I have dreamed of him.

'Already before I had upwound
The loosened ends of my girl's hair,
Or my girl's breasts had come to the round,
He took me in a dismaying stare.

'Although I can no longer count
What lips of lovers I have kissed,
I ride for him still; mount and dismount.
But make me a stirrup of your wrist—

'Tonight my shoulder shall be laid
With pressure, with longing, against your own,
Till my disquiet is allayed;
And you sleep; and I mount and ride on.

1922

TO HELEN

"I salute you in the spirit of copulation"
    —Cyril Tourneur's *Atheist's Tragedie*

After a certain period,
Regretful nights and lonely days,
I bought a woman made by God
From the models of Gaston Lachaise.

Danaë in her tower of brass
Was pitted by the golden rain;
About the middle of the Mass
The bishop's mitre writhed in pain.

An elephantress and a pard
Were wedded in a tropic stream.
The pachydermos panted hard,
The male brought forth a monstrous dream.

The golden Ind was not enough
For Alexander, so he wept.
Ah, when will come my own true love,
The flame-encircled nympholept?

1923

A SMALL ORATION TO THE SUN

When first I stretched out naked hands
You wrapped me in gilded swaddling bands;

You trained my body to grow tall
Leaning against your light as a wall.

A boy I felt the virginal dark pain
Of Danaë, and the golden dinting rain.

You blew my limbs like glass until I stood
Shining and clear, rosy with blood.

But now, O Sun, I have lain with the night
And am no more goodly in your sight.

I have limped so long under the moon
I am starched whiter than a ruffed buffoon;

The night has gone into my blood. O take
Pity on me for the old vow's sake

When stripling, ruddy and free I bowed
Under the shadows of the laurel wood

And saw the candid and austere dawn
Brighten, and cried: Before ten years are gone

I shall have ridden the high windy courses
And reined the snortings of the cloudy horses,

A lonely arrogant charioteer,
Green laurels weighing on the burnished hair!

The time is over. I should be glad
For the anger and the tan I had.

I am not Phaeton, but John Peale
Bishop, trailing a broken heel.

And I can no longer, silent, aspire
Toward your blue, hard brutal fire.

O plunge toward me, as a diver hurls
Him downward through a seagreen night of pearls.

1923

SONG

Who is there to defame her
    Although she is faithless?
I have heard no man name her
    But at once he was breathless
To say that the beauty she has
Is more terrible than white brass.

And no woman can blame her
   That she's no roof to cover
Her head and cannot long tame her
   Heart, her hoyden heart, to one lover:
Because her life is set on the rack
For no man, but for a song's sake.

1923

ALWAYS FROM MY FIRST BOYHOOD

Always, from my first boyhood,
I have known how, lying awake in a straightened
Nakedness—curtains of rain drawn at the window—
To summon from dimness beautiful bodies,
While, over my iron pallet, the painful
Windiness of lilacs spread an
Impalpable coverlet.

Bodies of young men centaured on horses:
Pliant and tawny as leopards, they ride
Over a ground made spongy by April and rains,
Against the drawn lines of a forest
Misty as rain, clouded with torn green;
Their thighs are pressed like bronze to the gleaming
White flanks of the horses; stirrupless, their feet
Toe in abandon; for their eyes are upraised
Where, blue and afar, the jutted mountains
Renew their ancient march in sunrise.

Scarcely has the brittle bickering of twigs
Subsided from their hoofbeats, when I have, with words,
Disenchanted from the grey web of the wood's edge
The tenuous, rose-frosted beauty of women.

264

Their mouths are claret-wet from some mystery,
Virginal, awful, performed in the forest;
Or else they have seen, by the yellow flame of crocuses,
The flushed and long-sought touching of lovers.
For now, with burnt savage hair outshaken,
Tremulous, exulted, they front the east wind,
Complaining toward the curveting fading horsemen.

Always it is the same: the fixed, blue-radiant
Mountains; the horsemen on horses, the young men
Staring afar off, and the women crying, crying—
The retreating lure and the sinuous beautiful bodies.

So, beginning at midnight, I am as one
Steeped in intolerable wine, and lie
Throbbing; exhausted only when the arid dawn
Cracks its light on the fissile planes of the mirror.

1923

"FOUR YEARS WERE MINE AT PRINCETON"

Four years were mine at Princeton,
    And the friends I had were four;
Though a man be wise as I am not
    And rich as I am poor,
And all his years be good to him
    He shall not find him more.

There was one had joy of colors,
    And one whose heart was wrung
By all the ancient beautiful things
    Which dead men have sung,
But all were filled with the fulness of life,
    For all were young.

265

One held with the great world gone,
  And one with the world we see,
One believed in the goodness of God,
  And one that no gods be;
But all had faith in the wisdom of youth;
  The men who were young with me.

There are better men among the dead,
  And better men will start
Out of the years which are not yet
  To match them part for part,
But these I wear as a signet set,
  As a seal upon my heart.

1917

TEDIUM

The moon, like a white-foot girl
Stirs the dark pool of the sky
To a froth and foam of cloud . . .

The hideousness, the filth, and the mud,—
All are hidden now.
And I remember hours when the war
Was something more than an interchange of days
And a dull procession of nights.

Do you remember?—a night when we two walking
Talked of the hopes of men,
Of old worlds clashing and new worlds born,
And all the while beauty went sighing
Through the dim paths and branches of our minds.

UNPUBLISHED EARLY POEMS
1914-1923

UNPUBLISHED EARLY POEMS

"IF DEATH SHOULD TIP CLOSE . . ."

If Death should tip close in a shift or magenta
   With folds of flame scarlet flung from her shoulder
And looped with a silver cord to cool its shadows:
If he would but press into my hands
From lean hands some sleepy poison
Dripped from laurel stalks or scales of insects—
I would say: Let me walk with you a while,
That I may see, Death,
If among all those lusty courteous ladies
Committed to vaults and the unenlightened worms
There be any like to my lady
So shining in body and so dark in mind.

Cir. 1920

"I HAVE ALREADY SEEN HER HEAD SO BOWED'

I have already seen her head so bowed
With inner loneliness, and the sun
Disgilded so of its high light, one would have said
So looked, so must have looked, that queen,
Berengaria, when, in a town of Maine, she heard
That Richard had gone forth again
With all his followers, toward the Saracens,
So noble her chagrin, so sunk her head.

Cir. 1920

SELF-PORTRAIT *

A glistening display of odorless pomade.
Blond hair urbanely parted. A front too broad,
Which in some happier generation might have shone
Proudly with laurels of unwithered green.

Eyes meaningless and grey, disposed to tears
While life remains so lovely and obscene.
Gross lips, priapic. Crooked nose and ears
Alert to Shelley, Dante and Verlaine.

Four limbs cylindrical, discreetly clothed
By Brooks in browns and Anglo-Saxon greys;
Yet underneath the straight thighs of a faun,
A torso maladroit and eagerly male.

At heart a man already centuried
When Troilus saw the threatened towers of Troy,
Or it may be a burning archangel
Whose plumes were shrivelled in Satanic wars.

1920

THE GRAVEDIGGERS

The gravedigger said, the old one:
    Let's stop, I'm all out of breath;
And the younger one said, If we stop now
    We'll never catch up with death.

The gravedigger said, the old one:
    It's cold on my neck like a breath;
Keep going, the younger shovelled,
    You've got to keep up with death.

Cir. 1920

* Mr. Edmund Wilson informs me that this poem is one of three self-portraits, the two others having been written by Miss Edna St. Vincent Millay and Mr. Wilson himself at the same time.

THE OLD MEN

Well, if I might this morning have risen and found
    All the old men, the crafty, secure and wise,
Dead in a bloody dust or windily drowned
    And the hard seas scraping the lids of their rigid eyes!

I am sick of their gentle whips and sick to the soul
    Of their noble guile and exalted avarice.
I have seen their restless hands and prefer on the whole
    The fidgeting twitch of a beggar scratching his lice.

Cir. 1921

ONLY THE SPRING RETURNS

This green and burgeoned youth
Being by spring refused
Grew of his greenness loath.

Then summer through green suffused
All laughed in excellence
No light nor dark accused.

Masking the sphere's advance
Leaves hid what autumn learns
In a single naked glance.

Seasons return. Mind burns
For beauty the body wore.
Only the spring returns.
All is unbalanced once more.

Cir. 1922

CAMP ZACHARY TAYLOR

DAY

Madness of geometricians.
The insomnia of countless carpenters made visible.
Monotony grown frenzied.
The spawn of Speed and Utility,
The cantonment in its vast hideousness
Sprawls on the ground,
And the vertical precision of smokestacks
Divide the sky.

NIGHT

Over all things the violet-shadowed snow,
Silence, and the star-delighted sky.
Before us the awful monotony of days
And the deep night without thought,
Without care.

January 5th,
   1918

THE PARADISE IN PEAT STREET

A year ago . . . and I knew where
Heaven was reached by a single stair . . .
A darkened chamber with peacock walls
And seven candles at intervals
(Burning dim as if for eyes
Not yet grown used to Paradise)
Seven candles and toast and tea
And most unholy jollity.
And if perchance there seldom came
Sackcloth saints or saints of flame,
There was an angel with red-burnt hair
Who read us snatches from Baudelaire,

An angel in a cloudlike dress
The color of ashes or nothingness,
Whom but to see was to be at once
Wiser than truths, older than suns.

Of all the Heavens of which I've heard
This was the one my choice preferred.
But if this too, like all the rest,
Lies darkened now and dispossessed
I can but guess. I only know
I may not go, I may not go,
Through the slippery street and up the stair,
Clatter the door and enter there
To sit at her lovely feet and be
A waif of immortality.

PRINCETON REVISITED

There were the towers of Princeton and the night
Made rich with darkened colours richly concealed—
The dark green of the yews and glimmering white
Dogwood. And suddenly something was mended
That broke in my heart, it is three years gone,
And the long truce with agony was mended,
And beauty was there, a splendor revealed,
After its shadow long dreamed upon.
And my heart that had been so long unfriended
Was suddenly brought to tears,
There in the night where its wound was healed
By its own bleeding and with tears.

Cir. 1922

THE MIRROR

A satyr coiled in silver dandles
    Young Anteros beside his knee;

273

Between a crooked flight of candles
My mirror wavers pallidly.

And there at night, with keys for wardens,
Naked and edged with suffused gold,
I sit and mark how my mouth hardens
Out of youth and is not yet old;

Reflect what cruel desire smoulders
In the blue pity of the eyes;
Observe the candor of the shoulders
And the sweet straightness of the thighs;

Make bare the scabby and unsightly
Gashes in my side, still unwhole;
Dry the smeared blood; and sometimes slightly
Preen the dragged plumage of my soul.

But lately in a lonely terror
I set the tapers at my back,
Peered round, and pressing to the mirror
Found my aureole black—black!

Cir. 1920

"I HAVE LIVED SO OFTEN"

I have lived so often the day of my return,
Made its minutes too fearfully my own,
That god himself does not know as I
The tickings and strikings of its hours.

It will be a day in autumn when
The pine trees cone alone in green.
It will be the red autumn when the days
Are a little sad for all their fallen gold.

274

It will be the end of an afternoon
When I shall turn into the little street
And the passers-by will say
That man has come close to his heart's desire.

I shall turn in through the gate
When the odor of dessicated leaves
That were fallen before the last rain
Is mixed with the bitter smell of box.

The door will open noiselessly. You are alone,
You do not hear. Your slender fingers
Are closed between the edges of a book,
And your heart holds the meaning of the last verses
        you have read.

All is as before. The clock ticks the minute.
The chessmen red and white stand on their squares.
The black and white harmonies of the spinet.

Slowly your eyes rest on my eyes,
And your astonished cry is stopped by a kiss,
A kiss long as the twilight, grateful as the night.

Then you hold me at the length of your arms
And say: My love, what have they done to you?
And I reply: Ah, but it was long
And again I feel your heart under my own.

Then I look around for the familiar things,
All is as before. The clock ticks the minute.
A harmony of old ivory sleeps in the spinet;
The chessmen are grave about their foolish squares.

I smell the comfortable smell of books.
And try the chairs and touch the wood
Then ask, thinking of the night before us,
Where have they put my Boccaccio?

Cir. 1921

"I LEAN UPON THE NIGHT"

I lean upon the night and count
The women who, unimplored, return,
Return on the night, and suddenly mount
The long stairs their sandalled feet have worn
Until my waiting nights must seem
Noble with phantoms as an ancestral dream.

One has been reared by blue-deep Italian ponds,
And moving keeps such equipoise
As though she had learned from bronze
Bright breast and slim thigh like a boy's;
She breathes as if it were her task
To make love brave, harlotry being a mask.

And how shall I speak calmly of her
Whose mind was like a bow pulled taut
And a burning arrow drawn to the ear?
Cruel or kind by whim, she brought
Such passion as queens bring to a slave,
Withholding in secret more than she gave.

The last is one most beautiful
Who glides before me noiseless as a cloud;
She has found upon the moon one pool,
One last unwithered pool, and bowed
To it with slim arms, and lifted up
Sweet poisons in a moon-moth colored cup.

These then I have loved in nakedness
Or wildly in thought, and had most joy
Of the harlot, most pain of the poetess;
But from her whom no word can decoy,
No sorcerous sound, to take up flesh again,
I have had all joy, all passion and all pain.

1921

MORNING IN DIJON

This balcony was wrought
Of fine iron of a man's thought.

In the street the noise
Begins of schoolward lagging boys.

Upon the bed she sleeps
And the dark sheet my imprint keeps.

I followed my desire.
And am refined in the sun's fire.

Cir. 1922